Curious SOMERSET

DERRICK WARREN

The
History
Press

First published in 2005 by Sutton Publishing Limited

Reprinted in 2009 by
The History Press
The Mill, Brimscombe Port,
Sroud, Gloucestershire, GL5 2QG
www.thehistorypress.co.uk

Reprinted 2010

British Library Cataloguing in Publication Data
A catalogue record for this book is available from the British Library.

ISBN 978- 0-7509-4057-3

Typeset in 11/13.5pt Janson.
Typesetting and origination by
Sutton Publishing Limited.
Printed and bound in England.

Contents

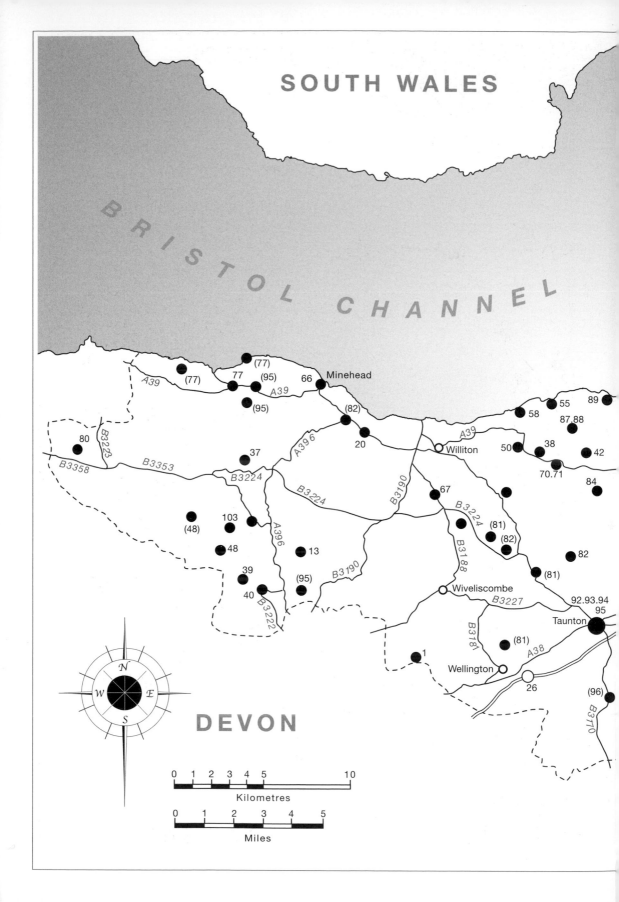

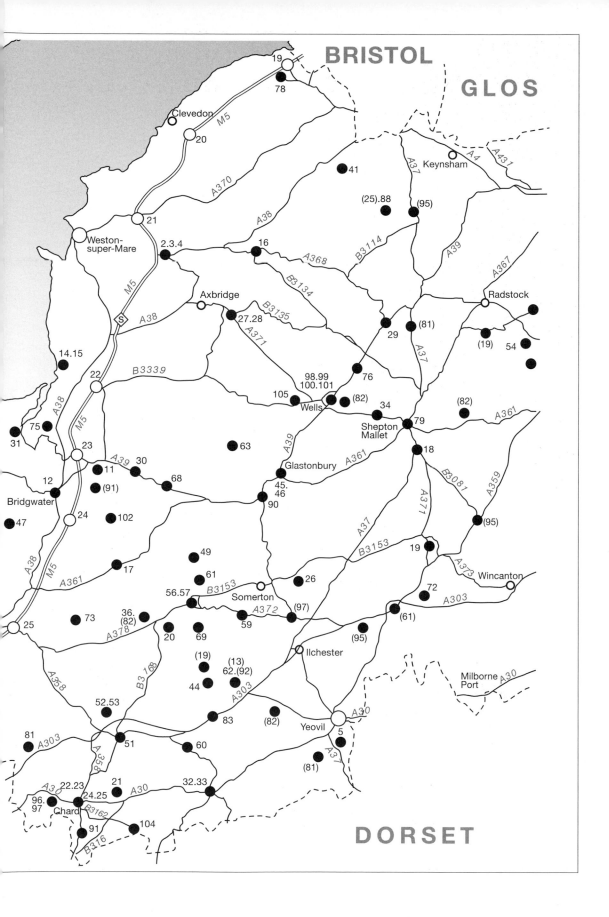

AUTHOR'S NOTE

Somerset is said to have the most diverse scenery of any county in Britain and it certainly has a great variety of unusual and curious features: from a forgotten spa to a Victorian fire station; from mud horses to a hobby-horse; from gutters to gorges and, on church walls, a female fertility figure to modern statuary, to say nothing of some odd customs and even odder characters. Some entries such as the Wells Clock and the Witch of Wookey are widely known, but are included because they are a unique part of Somerset. Some I had hoped to include, I found no longer existed – the glove weathervanes on Yeovil factories, for example – although I was more than compensated by finding, or had pointed out to me, other gems, including a watchman's hut in Bath, a church sanctuary ring and in Taunton County Museum, the 330-year-old 'murder weapon' used by a brave young girl – although I had known of this story I had always thought of it largely as a romantic fiction.

Because I was born and brought up in the county and later worked there as a (very inquisitive) Ordnance Surveyor, I knew of most of the subjects mentioned and it only needed a slight nudge to bring them to the surface of my memory. However, I did not know everything about them, so finding out became an extremely pleasant and rewarding exercise.

Churches I have largely passed over (they have been splendidly done by Pevsner and others) in favour of what they and their churchyards contain – for there history lies! Where a town or village is not mentioned, it does not mean that it holds nothing of interest, just that I did not know of it; neither, for the same reason, have I tried to balance the entries across the county. So this is a personal and idiosyncratic collection of unrelated stories of facts and places. For locals I hope I have jogged a few memories, and shown visitors something new of this delightful county.

The entries have been numbered in the alphabetical order of their location, with the prefix number corresponding to those on the location map. Most can be visited or seen from a public road or footpath, and the map references should enable them to be found easily (Ordnance Survey Landranger series, sheets 172, 181, 182, 183 and 193). However, even though a map reference is given it does not necessarily mean that there is public access – in those instances I have tried to make that clear in the text.

Except where individually acknowledged, all the photographs and illustrations are from my own collection.

Derrick Warren
Taunton, 2005

CURIOSITIES

ASHBRITTLE

The Old Yew

Because yew trees, *taxux baccata*, rot from their centres outwards but continue to grow and flourish around their circumference, in time becoming several separate trees, they are notoriously difficult to date accurately, for there are no ring circles.

The yew in the churchyard of St Andrew's at Ashbrittle is reputed to be the oldest living plant in the country, at over 3,000 years old. It has been conjectured that it was planted to mark either a holy place or a battle, but it is growing on the top of a small bowl barrow, which not only gives the yew an approximate age – Bronze Age of about 1000 BC – but also shows the significance of why the yew was planted there all those years ago – a pagan religious symbol for the person buried there. It was planted when Stonehenge was in use and was a venerable old tree when St Andrew's was founded, with the church being built nearby without disturbing the old belief.

No longer a solid tree, it now comprises seven trees growing in a circle 42ft in circumference, although each tree can clearly be seen as having once been part of the whole.

The base of the bowl barrow can be seen beneath the yew.

The split trunk.

William Wordsworth visited the old yew and in 1813 penned these lines:

> Of vast circumference and gloom profound
> This solitary tree a living thing produced too slowly
> Ever for decay of form and aspect.
> Too magnificent to be destroyed.

2

Map Ref
ST 394585

BANWELL

Beard's Stone

William Beard (1772–1865) was a farmer and amateur archaeologist who with other local enthusiasts explored a number of local caves, and collected the bones of animals that once lived in them. He delighted in the nickname 'Professor' and acted as guide to the many visitors who came out from Weston-super-Mare to visit the caves.

In 1842 Beard found an ancient human skeleton in a cave near Bishop's Cottage and, as a humanitarian gesture, had the remains buried on the west side of Caves Wood, at the end of an avenue of trees he had planted (now cut down), with this inscription:

A Human Skeleton Discovered near the Bishops Cottage
1842

Beard with his kindness brought me to this spot
As one unknown and long forgot
He made my grave and buried me here
When there was no kind friend to shed a tear
My bones are here but my spirit is fled
And for years unknown numbered with the dead
Readers as I am so shall you be
Prepare for death and follow me.

This was probably not an entirely altruistic gesture, for by all accounts
Beard 'thought not a little of himself'!

Beard's Stone.
(Roy Rice)

3

Map Ref
ST 399591

BANWELL

Fire-engine House

In East Street, near an old house named The Abbey, is the charming little Victorian fire-engine house with the following inscription carved in stone over the doors: 'This building is presented by Miss Elizabeth Fazakerly of Banwell Abbey and Fazakerly House, Lancashire, being the property of Banwell for ever to be used for the housing of the fire-engine belonging to that Parish. 19th Day of December 1887 in the year of the Jubilee of Her Most Gracious Majesty Queen Victoria.'

The fire-engine at that time was a wooden-wheeled, hand-drawn apparatus made in 1810 by James Manley of Redcliffe, Bristol, and bought by the parish of Banwell for £41 10*s*. It had twin reciprocating pumps of 4in bore and 8in stroke, and could deliver 44 gallons per minute to a height of 80ft from the long brass 'squirt' mounted on its top. It needed four men to work the pump and many volunteers forming a bucket chain to fill the reservoirs of the appliance with water.

Miss Fazakerly died early in 1888 but her sister honoured her gift; a trust eventually took over the building and because the architect

Fire-engine house
with a fire bell on
the chimney.

The fire-engine of 1810. *(Roy Rice)*

was far-sighted it was large enough to house more modern appliances, with retained firemen, until the 1960s. It had a rest room, now storing memorabilia of its life as a fire station, including the original pump which has been restored. The fire bell, used to call the brigade from its workplaces in the village when there was a fire, still hangs above the roof.

Similar manual pumps had engine houses at Bruton (ST 682347) and Castle Cary (ST 640321), but these were only large enough to house small pumps and, unlike that at Banwell, could not be adapted for larger, more modern appliances.

The little fire-engine house at Castle Cary.

BANWELL

The Turf Cross

Situated within a banked earthwork half a mile west of an Iron Age hill fort is a low mound (between 18in and 3ft high) in the shape of a cross. Both the cross and enclosure are now overgrown with trees and scrub, making them difficult to see and impossible to photograph. To add to these problems there is no consensus as to the age, origin or meaning of the cross, making it probably the most enigmatic archaeological site in Somerset.

One theory is that it might celebrate the birthplace of St Patrick, *c.* 387– *c.* 483. It is believed that he came from either the western counties of England or Wales, and much research has been done on the derivation of place names to try to determine his birthplace – Banwell being a strong contender. Similarly, where he died and lies buried is also shrouded in mystery, with great arguments arising within the Irish Church, for much kudos would have been attached to any church which could claim either.

Plan of the turf cross. *(Roy Rice)*

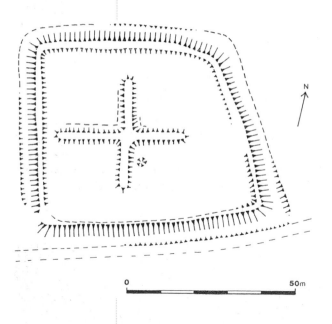

It is known that St Patrick had travelled widely between Britain and Ireland, so to aid his travels or to show the places he had visited, landmarks were erected around the coast. These consisted of roughly shaped, tall stone columns with the cross of St Patrick on their tops, painted white and set on a mound or platform to make them more visible.

When a geophysical survey was carried out on the Banwell cross some years ago it was hindered by the large Wellingtonia fir tree growing in the centre of the cross. The readings indicated a disturbance in the soil greater than the roots warranted, possibly indicating a hole large enough to have once held such a column. There is only one other turf cross in Britain and that is at Carn Ingle, near Fishguard in Wales, although platforms have been located which might have served the same purpose.

The prosaic answer to this conundrum, however, might be the one favoured by the then Royal Commission for Historic Monuments and the Somerset Sites and Monuments Record, that the cross was an elaborate pillow mound – an artificial mound of earth provided for rabbits (before they proliferated so widely over the countryside) to make a suitable site for a warren. In that case why is this warren in the shape of a cross, making it difficult to drain, for rabbits do not like damp areas? During a much earlier survey of the site a trench was dug across one of the arms of the cross that revealed it was composed largely of stones, which would have made it extremely difficult for the rabbits to make their burrows.

It is most unlikely that any definite answer will ever be found for the purpose and meaning of this mysterious site. The whole area is in private woodland.

BARWICK

The Follies

The approach to Barwick from the Yeovil to Dorchester road is down a narrow lane which suddenly dives into a gloomy chasm, with sheer 30ft-high sandstone cliffs, before emerging by the church. Perhaps it was this that in the 1820s inspired George Messiter of Barwick House, to build his four extraordinary structures, for each reaches up to the sky and the light. Barbara Jones, however, in her *Follies & Grottoes* (1974), puts them, from pictorial evidence, as fifty years earlier. It is said that they were built on the periphery of the Messiter estate; that is as may be, but seen on a map they form a cross, each one

5

Map Ref
ST 557137

Below, left to right: the Fish Tower, the Steeple or Cone and the Obelisk.

at the four points of the compass, with Barwick House in the centre. All are intervisible, although not now from the house as they are obscured by trees.

To the north is the Fish Tower (ST 561148), so called for the fish weathervane it once possessed. It is completely cylindrical, being 50ft high and 8ft in diameter. It is built of rough rubble stone and its hollow centre is 3ft across and lit by five oblong openings. There are no stairs or steps, but protruding stone makes it climbable for the extremely foolhardy!

Jack the Treacle Eater.

The structure to the west, the Cone (ST 556142), almost defies description. On a 4ft-high, 8ft-diameter solid circular base, three arches (the fourth side is solid) support a tapering steeple or cone, with small openings all the way up, something like a dovecote except that there is nothing inside. It rises to 80ft and is surmounted by a stone ball. There were once metal grills or railings in the arch openings.

The Obelisk (ST 559130) to the south is at the end of the longest arm of the cross and is in a small spinney. It is triangular and rises to 60ft.

It is, however, the structure to the east which is the oddest of them all. On the top of a 30ft-high arch, built from even larger rubble stone, sits a little circular stone tower with a conical stone roof, on the top of which is the winged figure of Mercury, the messenger of the gods. There is a blocked-up door to the little tower but no steps leading up to it, just the rough projections of the stones forming the arch. This is Jack the Treacle Eater (ST 566143). Legend has it that Jack lived in the tower and ran messages to London for the Messiter family, keeping fit by eating treacle! Only someone extremely agile could possibly gain access to the door, by climbing up the stones of the arch. There is a semicircular ha-ha in front of the arch and a deep-sunken, overgrown lane at the rear.

There are no records showing the true origin of any of the towers – only myth and speculation. All have footpaths nearby and the Obelisk has one leading directly to it.

BATH

Allen's Sham Castle

The city of Bath owes its beauty primarily to the ambitious planning of John Wood (the Elder) and his son John (the Younger) and to the energy and support of their friend and colleague, Ralph Allen (1694–1764).

Allen became extremely wealthy from being Post Master at Bath and reorganising the postal services of the area, which brought him £12,000 a year, and from his quarries, the easily worked white stone of which so enhances the appearance of Bath. Before he built his magnificent house above Bath, Prior Park, he had lived in Lilliput Alley, close to the Post House. From his windows he could see the bare Hambdon Hill, so in 1762 he thought he would improve his view by building a castle upon what is now Bathwick Hill, under the direction of his Clerk of Works, Richard Jones. Seen from the front the castle is impressive, for it is 100ft long and 40ft high, with an arched gateway flanked by round gate towers, embrasures, windows and cross-slits and, at each end, square towers. There are battlements all along the top. However, it is another picture entirely when seen

Allen's sham castle.

The rear of the
sham castle.

from the rear: the round turrets are mere semicircles, the towers
empty and all the windows and embrasures blind. Like a film set
or theatre 'flats', it is indeed a sham castle. It was acquired by the
city council in 1921 and is now floodlit at night, when it becomes a
fairytale castle. There is a footpath leading to it from North Road or
by car to Bath Golf Club.

Bath today owes a great deal to Ralph Allen for, as a contemporary
said on his death, 'he was an enlightened, generous and humane man'.

7

Map Ref
ST 737676

BATH

Beckford's Tower

William Beckford (1760–1844) became an extremely rich young man
when he inherited the estate at Fonthill, in Wiltshire, so giving him
the means to indulge his tastes in writing, music and the arts and,
above all, in building a magnificent new house for himself, the Gothic
Fonthill Abbey. This had a 276ft tower at its centre which was to have
been surmounted by a 174ft spire, bringing the edifice to a staggering
450ft; however, before the spire could be added the foundationless

tower collapsed in 1822, bringing the house down with it. Because of mounting debts, Beckford had fortunately sold Fonthill two years previously for £330,000 (in his own words, 'advantagiously') and moved to Bath.

Here Beckford lived at 20 Lansdown Crescent and he acquired a mile-long narrow strip of land behind his house, leading up to the top of Lansdown Hill, which he landscaped and made into a beautiful garden. At the top he built another tower. (He was obsessed with towers and once said, 'Some people drink to forget their unhappiness. I do not drink, I build. And it ruins me.') This 154ft-high tower with a small house at its foot was completed in 1827 and designed by H.E. Goodridge.* It served not only as Beckford's study but housed the magnificent collection of books and art that this relatively impoverished sybarite still owned.

Beckford's Tower.

The tower has been called neoclassical, but for its first 100ft it is just square and rather plain, even dull. Then comes the parapet and observation room/study with three tall windows on each of its four sides, crowned by a replica of the Lysicrates Choragie monument in Athens. However, this lantern or cupola is made of oak with cast-iron columns, and had until recently been painted a drab brown; this has now been stripped off and the whole gilded as it had been in Beckford's day. This lifts the tower from being somewhat sombre to being almost beautiful.

During the 1840s the surrounding garden became a cemetery and the house a mortuary chapel; the cemetery now is similar to Highgate in London, with fascinating old tombstones and memorials, all rather overgrown – the difference being the view. Beckford was eventually buried there in a Scottish granite sarcophagus (designed by himself) at one end of an oblong mound surrounded by a ha-ha. The other (empty) end of the mound is thought to be the burial place of Beckford's favourite dog.

After many vicissitudes the tower and cemetery are now owned by the Bath Preservation Trust and open to the public at weekends and on public holidays, while the house is leased to the Landmark Trust as holiday accommodation. The cemetery is always open.

* Although Goodridge and James Wyatt at Fonthill were nominally Beckford's architects, his own input was great – unfortunately at Fonthill with disastrous effect.

BATH

Pulteney Bridge

8
Map Ref
St 751648

In the eighteenth century William Johnstone married an heiress, Frances Pulteney, and planned a new estate of grand houses at Bathwick on the meadows of the south bank of the Avon. He engaged a friend and fellow Scot, architect Robert Adam, to plan the estate and the new bridge that would be needed to connect it to Bath. Adam designed the bridge as a variation of Palladio's design for the Ponte di Rialto in Venice. Johnstone's grand plans for Bathwick never materialised, but his bridge survives as the only example in Bath by that great architect. The westernmost pier of the bridge, however, collapsed in about 1790 because of poor foundations, and had to be rebuilt.

Pulteney Bridge had no houses on it, just two rows of narrow shops as there are today and, as now, they would have been exclusive shops, catering for the rich and famous. Unlike today, the shops' patrons would then have had to pay for their visit, for tolls were charged to cross the bridge, and the little domed pavilions at each end of the bridge were once the tollhouses. It is a great pity that the bridge is not, or cannot be, pedestrianised for that would restore it to its former glory.

One of the
tollhouses.

Pulteney Bridge
from downriver.

BATH

Sally Lunn's

9
Map Ref
ST 750646

In 1680 Solange (Soli) Luyon came to England as a young Huguenot refugee, finding employment with a baker in Lilliput Alley, Bath, and bringing with her the recipe for the French brioche-style bread and buns. Eventually she took over the bakery and anglicised her name to Sally Lunn, with the rich, round buns that she made, and the bakery itself, taking her name.

In 1704 Queen Anne came to Bath to take the waters and thus sparked off the city's popularity, becoming the hub of the social whirl with public breakfasts, teas and suppers, balls and musical occasions. As was said at the time, Bath became a centre of 'busy idleness' and 'the constant doings of nothings'! Sally Lunn's became the 'in place' for afternoon teas, patronised by the likes of Beau Nash, for which the well-to-do paid a shilling for 'Tea and Cake' (a Sally Lunn) – a vast sum, when that was a day's wage for a farm labourer.

The premises occupied by Sally Lunn's has always a bakery or tearooms, and is now known to be the oldest building in Bath, having been built in 1482 on the site of a Benedictine monastery, although the exterior has since been altered. For many years the original recipe for a 'Sally Lunn' was lost, but in the 1930s it was found in a basement cupboard, and is now part of the deeds of the property.

The ground and first floors are now the tearooms, but the original kitchen and bread oven of the bakery in the basement have been restored and now form a small museum, free to the public, and where Sally Lunns can be bought – they are truly delicious with clotted cream and raspberry jam!

Sally Lunn's teashop.

BATH

Watchman's Box

Like any other eighteenth-century city with a large well-to-do population, Bath had its share of criminals: footpads, 'dips', burglars and worse. This was before the days of 'peelers' and 'bobbies' so watchmen were employed, especially at night, to protect the citizens and their property.

The watchmen were provided with small, round, stone huts (8ft 6in high by 4ft 6in across) in which they could shelter from the elements yet still guard the area for which they were responsible. There was a curved wooden door and no doubt the watchmen had an occasional quiet pipe and perhaps a snooze!

These watchmen's huts were once all over Bath, but this one from about 1793, on the green at the junction of Norfolk Crescent and Nelson Place, is now the sole survivor.

Watchman's box.

BAWDRIP

The Dwarf's House

11
Map Ref
ST 342395

Why this little house is the size it is will never be known, for it would fit easily into most living rooms. Its external measurements are 13ft long, 9ft wide and 13ft to the apex of the roof; there is a second floor, a fireplace and a door which is only 4ft 10in high. It must have been built for someone to live in comfortably, but in the 1970s local people could only vaguely remember its last occupants: a married couple, the husband being 6ft 2in tall, of whom it was said – with country humour – that he had to come outside to put his coat on.

But perhaps Bawdrip is best known for the sad Christmas story, the 'Mistletoe Bough'. On 14 June 1681 Eleanor Lovell was married in St Michael's Church; at the wedding feast, tired of dancing, the guests decided to play hide and seek. Eleanor sped away, not to be found, in spite of a prolonged search, until a Christmas many years later when an old chest, tucked away in the furthermost corner of the old house, was opened. Inside was Eleanor's skeleton in her mouldering wedding clothes. All this is recorded on a stone tablet inside the church and there is a copy in the porch. But for a real tear-jerker, read Thomas Hayne Bayly's Victorian poem, The Mistletoe Bough (1884), two verses of which are shown below:

Dwarf's house.

They sought her that night, they sought her
   next day,
They sought her in vain when a week
   passed away.
In the highest, the lowest, the loneliest spot,
Young Lovell sought wildly, but found her
   not.

At length, an old chest that had long laid
   hid
Was found in the castle; they raised the lid.
A skeleton form lay mouldering there
In the bridal wreath of that lady fair.

15

Map Ref
ST 304494

BURNHAM-ON-SEA

The Spa

The eighteenth and early nineteenth centuries were the golden age of the English spa – Buxton, Cheltenham, Harrogate, Malvern and, above all, Bath. Spa treatments were so popular that many smaller and less fashionable towns, should they have any kind of medicinal spring, 'cashed in' on the vogue. Burnham (the 'on-Sea' was not added until the early twentieth century) could offer seabathing, a very popular treatment during the early nineteenth century, and the local curate, the Revd David Davies, saw the possibilities offered by this and the existence of two medicinal springs close to the town and beach. In 1829 Davies built a Pump House close to the sulphurous and the saline springs, an imposing Bath House and Assembly Rooms, and several 'villas' where those 'taking the cure' could stay. External mud treatment was also given, for the silt (mud) deposited along the coast by the rivers draining the Somerset Levels became rich with sea-borne minerals and was considered extremely efficacious in the treatment of some ailments.

The well and
bathhouses,
c. 1840.
(Bob Thomas)

The doorway at
Capland Spa.

Burnham, however, could offer little in the way of other entertainment. So when advances were made in medical knowledge and there was a gradual decline in the use of spa treatments; by the mid-seventeenth century the spa at Burnham was no longer a viable business, and closed. Although the Pump House and the springs have gone, Davies would recognise the rest of his development today. The villas are still there with two bearing their original names – Myrtle House and Cottage – while the imposing four-storeyed Bath House and Assembly Rooms is now Steart House. When Mr Davies built his complex there was no promenade – just a pathway across the 'sand-tots' (dunes) – so everything was built to face inland, across the once extensive pleasure gardens, with their backs to the sea.

There are medicinal springs all over Britain and two of these in Somerset became spas: at Horwood, near Wincanton (ST 724272), the Well House survives; and, although the well and bath house have both gone, at Capland Spa (ST 301190) near Hatch Beauchamp, its name can still be seen carved on the stone arch over the door.

16
Map Ref
ST 476587

BURRINGTON

Rock of Ages

Burrington Combe is a pretty, densely wooded, steep-sided valley with the road winding gently up to the top of the Mendips. There are rocks scattered among the trees and, near the bottom by the car park, is a sloping mass of rock on its eastern side.

It is, however, the huge rock on the other side of the combe, with a great split right down through it, that has become so well known – the Rock of Ages.

In 1762 the Revd Augustus Toplady, curate at the neighbouring village of Blagdon, was walking in the combe when he was overtaken by a violent thunderstorm. He took refuge in this cleft in the rock, and while the storm raged he composed that universally known hymn which begins:

> Rock of Ages, cleft for me,
> Let me hide myself in thee.

Rock of Ages.

BURROW BRIDGE

The Mump

17
Map Ref
ST 359305

Rising 75ft above the Somerset Levels east of the River Parrett, Burrow Mump looks something like a smaller version of Glastonbury Tor: both are of the same geological formation with a core of lias and marl; both have the ruins of a religious building on their summits and the same dedicatory name – St Michael. Burrow Mump was, in Anglo-Saxon, a 'tot-eyot' (lookout island) and a 'tutte-yate' (lookout and gateway). King Alfred used it as a defensive position against the Danes, for it was near the bridge over the River Parrett and had causeway paths across the 'moors' to the Island of Athelney and to Aller. There was a chapel on its summit during the reign of Edward IV (1461–83), and in 1652 mention is made of the Mump with its 'Free Chapel of St Michael at Burrowe on the top'. In 1645, during the Civil War, the ruined chapel was garrisoned with 120 men for three days by the Royalist, Goring, in defence of Langport, which was being attacked by the Commonwealth army under Fairfax. One hundred years later the chapel was recorded as a ruin; rebuilding commenced in 1793 but it was never completed, so what is seen today is much as it was left then, a partly built church. In 1946 the owner, Major A.G. Barrett, gave Burrow Mump to the National Trust as a county memorial to the dead of the Second World War.

Whether one believes in ley lines or not, the Mump has a strange connection with one such – the longest in Britain. Commencing at St Michael's Mount in Cornwall, the ley line crosses Brent Tor in Devon, the Mump and Glastonbury Tor in Somerset, Avebury in Wiltshire, then on across England until it finishes at the sea near Caistor in Norfolk. Every church either directly on this line or very close to it is dedicated to St Michael, and a computer programme, using 5km coordinates, has shown this line to be true. Is it a colossal coincidence or is it something else?

St Michael's on the Mump rising above the floods, *c.* 1922, from Dunmonia and the valley of the River Parrett.

18

Map Ref
ST 628417

CANNARD'S GRAVE

The name of the crossroads, Cannard's Grave, and hence the nearby inn, stems from an occurrence that happened over 400 years ago, although over the years there have been variations to the story.

One goes that Kenred (Cannard?), a pagan, was uncle to King Ina who had converted to Christianity, but when Kenred died he was buried where he died, as was the custom. Another story refers to a Giles Cannard, an innkeeper, who, needing money, resorted to forgery to obtain it. He was found out and the disgrace drove him to suicide, so he was buried at a crossroads, as all suicides were.

However, the most likely story is that recorded by John Billingsby in his *General View of the Agriculture of the County of Somerset*, commissioned by the Government and published in 1795. He was discussing the difficulties experienced by sheep farmers on the Mendips, including the prevalence of sheep stealing, and went on to say 'an inn sign shows a man hanging from a gallows with a sheep nearby. This is known as Cannard's Grave after a highwayman (thief) – some say the landlord of the inn – who lived there about 200 years ago. It is said he was arrested for sheep stealing, tried, condemned and was then hanged on the village green and later buried at the porch of the inn, outside what is now the smoke-room window'. As this was recounted 210 years ago, local memories would have been more recent and possibly nearer the truth. The inn sign still shows a man hanging from a gallows, with other men drinking nearby, regardless of the grim reminder swinging above them.

19

Map Ref
ST 640323

CASTLE CARY

The Lock-up

The little round lock-up (there are only three other round lock-ups in the country) is in the middle of the square above the Market House and is 10ft high and 7ft in diameter; it has no windows, only two ventilators under the eaves. It was built in 1779 by the lord of the manor, costing £23, the money being taken from two local charities: one set up in 1605 by David Llewellin, a local 'churugeon', who gave £10 for the 'use of the poor forever', and the other, at about the same date, by John Francis, who gave the interest on £2 for the same cause. In 1922 the current lord of the manor, Sir Henry Hoare Bart, generously gave the building to the parish council. It was used principally for overnight stays by those too inebriated to go home, but

from 1785 any child caught playing truant from Sunday school was incarcerated there until the lessons finished. Could this now be an old solution to an perennial problem?

The square lock-up at Kilmersdon (ST 696522), now used as a bus shelter, was built in 1785 for slightly less than the one at Castle Cary – £22 13s 2d. Parish records reveal that in 1786 the beadle was paid 5d beer money for his trouble in locking up Charles and John Abraham and, a year later, 4d for doing the same to a soldier. The lock-up became known as the 'Blind House' because of its lack of windows, and the one at Mells (ST 726490) was also known by that name. Neither the one at Castle Cary nor another at Kingsbury Episcopi (ST 433210) were ever referred to as Blind Houses. The lock-up at Kingsbury Episcopi is octagonal, constructed entirely of dressed Hamstone and sits in the middle of the village green. Its inmates did have light, for high in the walls are two 1ft by 5in wide stone slits, but even though so small, each has an iron bar down its centre so that nothing could be passed through.

Above, left: The lock-up, Castle Cary.

Above, right: The 'blind house' at Kilmersdon.

Below: Kingsbury Episcopi.

20
Map Ref
ST 009424/
ST 405247

CARHAMPTON/DRAYTON

Wassailing

The names Somerset and cider are synonymous, and although not so widespread as formerly, the county still has many old cider orchards and farms making their own cider (but no longer as payment for their workers). The old varieties of bitter-sweet cider apples continue

to be grown – Kingston Black, Yarlington Mill and Redstreak – together with the sweeter Tom Putt and Colebrook to take the edge off the rough cider. Sadly, most of the old customs and traditions of cider-making (and drinking) have died out. Wassailing, however, is still actively carried on in two villages: Carhampton in West Somerset and Drayton, some 11 miles east of Taunton. The word 'wassail' comes from the Anglo-Saxon 'waes hael' meaning 'health to you' and the ceremonies take place around Twelfth Night, Christmas time and on 'old Twelfth Night' – 17 January. Two forms of wassailing survive, to the apple-tree and the house-to-house, of which the apple-tree ceremony is undoubtedly the older.

Behind the Butcher's Arms Inn at Carhampton, it is the apple tree that is venerated. At midnight on 17 January the company goes to an old cider-apple tree in the orchard behind the inn, a piece of toast, soaked in cider, is placed on a branch as an offering to the good spirits, and the wassailing song is sung:

Doorway to an old cider house, enlarged to take hogsheads, not its corpulent owner!

Old apple tree we Wassail thee
And happily thou will bear
For the Lord doth know where we shall be
Till apples another year.
To bloom well, to bear well,
So merry let us be
Let every man take off his hat
And shout out to th'old apple tree:
Old apple tree we Wassail thee
And hoping thou will bear
Hat full, cap full, dree bushel bags full
And a little heap under the stair.
Hip, Hip, Hurrah!

A shotgun is then fired up through the branches of the tree to frighten away the evil spirits, cider is drunk and merrymaking proceeds! The old pagan custom of tree-worship is clearly evident and being in wintertime near the solstice, can be linked to the mistletoe, of which the apple tree is so often the host.

The Drayton wassail entailed visiting the houses of the better-off – the vicar, the squire and the farmers. That great collector of folk songs, Cecil Sharp, recorded the Drayton wassail song in 1903 and he predicted that in a few years the tradition would have died out. Although never having previously been written down, it survived, passed on through oral tradition, and is a rare example of a living English folk song. It is still evolving, as this version of 1977 shows, of which the second and third verses have been omitted:

> Chorus   Wassail, O, Wassail, all over the town;
>   The cup it is white and the ale it is brown;
>   The cup it is made of the good ashen tree,
>   And so is the beer of the best barley.
>
>   For it's your wassail and it's our wassail
>   And I'm jolly come to our jolly wassail.
>   So no harm, boys, harm; no harm, boys, harm;
>   And a cup of good cider will do us no harm.
>
> Chorus   . . .
>
>   We've not come here for to eat or to drink
>   But to keep up the custom until another year.
>
> Chorus   . . .

At each 'wassailed' house the leader stands to the right of the door with the rest in a semicircle before the hosts. The song ends and the leader steps forward and gives a toast: 'God bless Master and Mistress and all the family' and the season's greetings. The group are then entertained with drinks and by giving money, now usually a donation to a village charity.

Sharp speculated that this form of 'wassailing' had originated at the time of the Norman Conquest, but is now thought to have started in the seventeenth century as a way for labourers to earn a few extra pennies (and drinks) at Christmas time. Long may the custom continue!

21
Map Ref
ST 353091

CHAFFCOMBE

Avishayes House Clock Tower

The mellow red-brick, eighteenth-century Avishayes House is overlooked from the north-east by a grassy, lightly wooded eminence known as Castle Hill. Near the summit is a squat, square, castellated

brick tower, surmounted by a white-painted, elegantly slender clock and bell tower. The whole harmonises so well with the house and its surroundings that it is a surprise to learn that it is comparatively modern.

The late nineteenth-century brick tower once contained tanks supplying the house with water pumped up by a hydraulic ram from a spring lower down the hill. The clock tower erected on its top only dates from 1985, with the design of the timber and lead-covered cupola inspired by the cupola on Old Blundell's School in Tiverton, Devon. It was constructed by a local building firm, R.G. Spiller of Chard, under the supervision of the leading classical architect of the day, Philip Jebb. The nineteenth-century single-faced turret clock and carillon came originally from Highclere Castle in Hampshire, but was found in a sad condition at Ilchester.

Clock tower at Avishayes.

22
Map Ref
ST 320086

CHARD

The Bunker

In early 1938 the little market town of Chard (population then just over 4,000) was intrigued by the arrival of one of the country's largest constructional engineering companies, Sir Robert McAlpine & Sons, and all the mechanical equipment needed for a major building project. Curiosity became intense when they proceeded to excavate a huge hole in the back garden of the Westminster Bank (now the NatWest Bank) in Fore Street and the site of a former cottage in Combe Street. The entrance to the site was down the driveway to Springfield House, where the disruption drove its elderly owner to take his own life.

In the hole a great concrete, bomb-proof bunker was built, some 125ft by 82ft, its sides towering up to over 15ft above, and down to

Left: The bunker.

Below: One of its steel entrance doors.

a greater depth, below, ground. There were massive steel doors and 8ft of earth was replaced on the top, to give both added protection and provide the bank's manager with a garden once more, albeit an elevated one. The total cost was £60,000.

As can be imagined, rumour was rife as to its use when it was completed in August 1939, just before the war started. A depository for the crown jewels was the favourite, but the truth was more mundane: duplicate copies of the bank's customer records were kept there, updated daily, in the eventuality of Head Office in Threadneedle Street, London, being destroyed; but 'should these statements fall into unauthorised [German] hands the accounts will be identified by a code number only'. As the bunker had spare capacity, the emergency supply of banknotes for the Bank of England was held here until 1943. However, in response to a recent enquiry to the Tower of London, the Curator's office replied, somewhat enigmatically, 'I have asked our Head of Works of Art, who says that reputedly the Crown Jewels were stored in a slate mine in Wales, but there is no concrete evidence of this. I don't think their whereabouts has ever been officially confirmed.'

Now disused and too large a structure to be demolished without even greater disruption than when it was built, the bunker can be seen from the car park in Combe Street.

CHARD CAVES

A charter of 1235, outlining the limits of the borough of Chard, states 'on the west the "staunmasons"', so there must have been a quarry here then – probably an open working. As the band of fine sandstone, interspersed with layers of chert flint, dipped to the north-east, the quarry would have become progressively deeper until it was more economic to mine rather than remove the overburden. During the sixteenth century the mine would have been worked mainly for the chert flint, for when knapped square on one face, the flints made an attractive and hard-wearing building material. Fine examples of its use can be seen in Crimchard House, Chard Grammar School, the Manor House and the Court House, all of Fore Street, and the cottages now forming Chard Museum in the High Street.

The present cave is approximately 20ft below ground, 26ft wide, 12ft high and 40ft deep, sloping slightly downwards, with one supporting pillar still in place. It was originally far more extensive, but the first 100ft or so of the cave has collapsed (or been brought down deliberately) leaving a part of its north-west side and the stumps of two supporting pillars exposed. During the eighteenth century the present cave was used by Dissenters as a meeting place.

At the far end of the cave is a natural fissure, now blocked by a fall, and it was this fissure that no doubt gave rise to the stories of secret passages to Crimchard House or to the Manor House. It was somewhere down this fissure that during the late nineteenth century a man and his dog went exploring – the dog came out but the man didn't, for the rescuers could not get past a large fall of rock.

The caves are on private land.

Entrance to Chard caves.

CHARD

Street Gutters

24
Map Ref
ST 324086

For over 400 years Chard's main source of water came from three strong springs on the south side of the High Street, the surplus water flowing in gutters down both sides of the Cornhill and Fore Street and along the east side of Holyrood Street – as they still do. There is nothing particularly unusual in this for many towns have the same: Cheapside, Frome and the High Street, Wells, spring to mind. What is unusual in Chard's case is the fact that Chard lies on the watershed between the River Isle, which flows into the Bristol Channel, and the River Axe, which flows into the English Channel. The main street forms the watershed so that the gutter on the north side flows into the Bristol Channel while that on the south side flows into the English Channel. Alas, it is no longer entirely true, for at some time in the fairly recent past the mighty tributary of the Axe was diverted at the bottom of the town into the Isle. The gutter in Holyrood Street, however, still flows eventually into the River Axe, and they all continue to give infinite pleasure to those small children with anything to float down them!

Above: Gutter in Holyrood Street.

Left: The gutters down Fore Street, *c.* 1840.

climbing again to Green Down, a Somerset Wildlife Trust nature reserve. To the west of the track, standing about 50yds out all by itself in the rough pasture, is a small building, 12ft by 12ft, built of brick and dressed lias stone; there are no windows and the now doorless entrance has a similar, although much smaller, opening beside it – looking for all the world like sentry boxes for a soldier and his dog.

It has now been established that this was in fact a store for the dynamite and detonators used by the railway contractors excavating the huge cutting for the Great Western Railway's new line to London in 1903–5. It has been restored and is now maintained by the Somerset Wildlife Trust.

There is a similar little building, although not in nearly such good condition, on the hill above the long Somerton tunnel, constructed at the same time. This one is near Monday's Lane near Long Sutton (ST 467270).

27

Map Ref
ST 475543

The Lion Rock, Cheddar.

CHEDDAR

The Gorge

Cheddar Gorge is probably the best known natural feature in the British Isles and is certainly the most visited; it has been written about in countless publications and photographed from every conceivable angle, including the air. But nothing can adequately describe or give a true image of its awesome grandeur; it has to be a personal experience, and to be truly appreciated the great chasm must be approached and entered from the east. As the road winds downwards so the sides of the valley become deeper and steeper, the slopes become cliffs, the road has ever-tighter bends, and the cliffs become vertiginous with the impression of the earth closing in over the puny mortals and their cars. Suddenly the bottom is reached, the view opens out and there is Cheddar – with its caves, the milling throng of tourists, the jammed cars and innumerable shops and cafés.

For many years it was thought that there had been a huge river flowing in a vast cavern under the Mendips, and that after the last Ice Age the roof of this cavern had collapsed, forming the gorge. This would explain why the rocks on either side

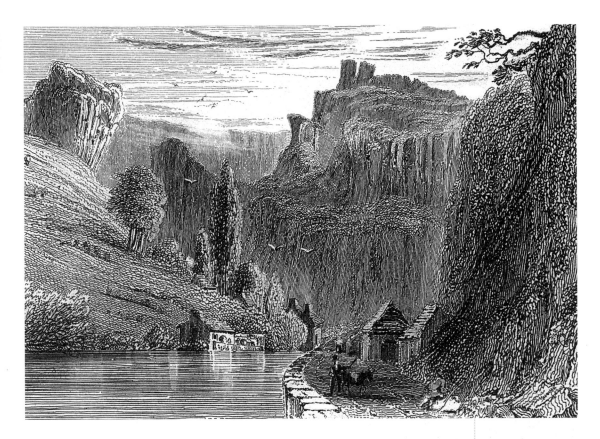

of the gorge are identical, which would not be the case if the gorge had been made by a cataclysmic shift in the earth's structure.

Current thinking, though, is that the original valley was cut out by a river long before the Pleistocene Age (50,000 years ago), but after that, the great quantity of water produced by the melting snow and ice could not penetrate the deep permafrost affecting this part of the country and so prevented any water percolating into the cracks and fissures of the rocks forming the Mendip Hills. This floodwater found a valley and, like flash floods still do in Colorado and elsewhere, gouged out a deep channel down which to pour, with Cheddar Gorge being the result. It is 1½ miles long and the highest cliff is over 450ft. The first historical mention of the gorge was when King Edmund (980–1016) nearly rode over its edge when out hunting in a thick mist – the deer was not so lucky! The Forest of Mendip was, in those days, a royal hunting ground.

Although not nearly as grand as the gorge at Cheddar, Ebor Gorge (ST 528488), just off the road from Wookey Hole to Priddy, has no cars and no hordes of tourists. It is a nature-lover's paradise to be walked in peace and utter quiet.

The Gorge,
c. 1850, from an
old print.

28
Map Ref
ST 465535

CHEDDAR

Jacob's Ladder and Observation Tower

Jacob's ladder and observation tower, *c.* 1930. The hillside is now wooded.

In about 1912 the 'lookout' was originally a wooden structure, but in the 1920s it was rebuilt with a steel frame and wood cladding on the outside. This cladding was removed in 2000 because visitors complained of feeling claustrophobic when climbing the forty-eight metal steps in the dark. Once at the top there are spectacular panoramic views across Somerset: to Glastonbury Tor and into Wiltshire; across Sedgemoor to the Blackdown and Quantock Hills, then over to the sea at Weston-super-Mare and Burnham-on-Sea, and on a clear day to Steep Holm and Flat Holm and the mountains of Wales.

But it isn't just those forty-eight steps that are needed to see this view. First there are the 274 steps of Jacob's ladder to be climbed from the village far below. The evenly spaced concrete steps have a handrail and there are seats at regular intervals on which those ascending can catch their breath. The steps are also the start of a 3-mile walk around the top of the Gorge. There is a fee.

29
Map Ref
ST 597531

CHEWTON MENDIP

The Frid Stool

Set into the window-ledge under the north window in the Sanctuary of St Mary Magdalene Church at Chewton Mendip is a Frith or Frid stool. 'This was a seat or chair, generally of stone, placed near the altar in some churches; this was the last and most sacred refuge for those who claimed privilege of sanctuary within them; and for the violation of which [privilege] the most severe punishment was deemed' – so says Parker's Glossary which is displayed inside the stool in the church.

True to form, scholars now postulate that this was merely a recess, probably an aumbry used for an Easter sepulchre, but the church goes back to Saxon times so the older belief is probably the true one.

Two other Frid stools are known: at Hexham in Northumberland, and Beverley in Yorkshire.

CHILTON POLDEN

The Priory

At Cock Hill the ridge of the Polden Hills narrows to little more than the width of the A39 (itself once a Roman road) and built under its north flank is Chilton Priory, the roof of which is almost level with the road and only a few yards from it. The Priory, once known facetiously as Stradling's Castle, does indeed look like an ecclesiastical building, but it was never that.

It was designed and started in about 1830 by William Stradling, an antiquarian of some repute and a 'snapper-up of unconsidered trifles'. This was the era of church restorations and what Stradling snapped up were the artefacts which the restorers pulled down or ripped out. The Priory reflects this, for it has a crenellated west tower, under which is a crypt, a nave, a south porch and an oratory at the east end. When completed, Stradling said 'it was erected as a repository for many curiosities which would otherwise have been destroyed'. These include the pinnacles from Langport Church tower; battlements and grotesque heads from Enmore Castle; a turret from Shepton Mallet; a gable finial from Chedzoy; stonework from Glastonbury Abbey; a monastery door; an iron-bound door from Stokecoursey; communion rails from North Petherton, and other items – all were ideal for Stradling to save and incorporate into his Priory.

Chilton Priory.

When it was finished in 1839 he filled it with curiosities from around the world and especially those items unearthed from 'the immense turbury' which he could see looking eastwards from the front of his home. When he died the contents were dispersed, except for local items, which went to Taunton Museum.

Of course, Stradling could never have envisaged the traffic which now roars by within feet of the Priory; it is still a private house but the feel of the building can be appreciated when seen from the road, if the traffic permits.

31
**Map Ref
ST 261422**

COMBWICH

Dolphins in the Parrett

Before Hinkley Point nuclear power station could be built on the coast near Stogursey, several major construction works had to be undertaken. The many narrow roads had to be widened, some having completely new stretches built to take the building materials and wide and heavy engineering equipment to the site. Much of this was to be brought in by sea to the little quay at Combwich on the River Parrett, which also had to be enlarged and strengthened. Although at high tide the Parrett is very deep, it is not particularly wide and there was little room in which to manoeuvre the ships to the quayside, which was beside a creek at right angles to the river.

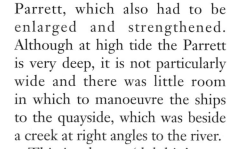

The dolphins at a medium tide.

This is where a 'dolphin' came in – a concrete platform against which a vessel could put her bow, to act as a fulcrum, while her stern was pushed round by a small tug-boat until she was broadside on to the river, enabling her to berth beside the quay. Dolphins are a common sight at many ports where open water is constricted, but unusual objects to see in a river such as the Parrett. At high tide they look like what they are intended to be – solid concrete 'islands' about 20ft long – but at low tide the tidal rise and fall can exceed 30ft, and the ones in the Parrett rear up naked out of the mud on their long steel legs, looking for all the world like space-age beings or, one can say, like fish out of water!

CREWKERNE

The Clock Stopped

32
Map Ref
ST 439097

On the inside west wall beneath the gallery of St Bartholomew's Church are two commemorative brasses. One is most poignant: it says 'to the Memory of Bridget, the daughter of John and Bridget Thomas, who lies buried near this place August 1723 in the 4th year of her Age'. While there is nothing unusual about that, it is the engraving above the words that wrings the heart: an engraved clock face with the hands pointing to 6.52 when, on the child's death, time must have stopped.

The other brass has a comic side, if the story relating to it is true; on the crest above the coat of arms of Adam Martin of Seaborough, who died in 1678, is a picturesque depiction of a monkey looking at itself in a hand mirror. This is supposed to have inspired a soap manufacturer to name one of his soaps 'Monkey Brand'. If true, he must have done so with tongue in cheek, for 'Monkey Brand' contained an abrasive powder and was used for very dirty jobs – and for the washing of inmates of workhouses on admittance. So who but a curious monkey would look in a mirror when using it?!

CREWKERNE

A Witch's Stone

33
Map Ref
ST 340092

Mary Ann (Nan) Bull was an itinerant trader – possibly a gipsy – selling small merchandise such as tinware, needles, muslin and ribbons. She travelled all over Somerset and Dorset during the latter part of the nineteenth century, going from place to place in a horse and wagon which carried not only her stock in trade but all her worldly goods, for she slept, summer and winter, beneath the wagon. She became disliked and feared, especially because of her tongue, calling down curses on those of whom she fell foul or those who would not buy her wares, particularly when she was in drink, as she often was.

Even in the more enlightened nineteenth century, country superstition and old beliefs were still strong and she became regarded as a witch. So when, on a bitter winter's day, she was found dead beneath her wagon, she was buried at this crossroads near Curriott Hill, just outside Crewkerne, and a stone put up to testify to the fact. It is reported that there was an inquest at Wincanton and that she was buried there in a pauper's grave. But why Wincanton, why was the stone erected where it is, and who went to that expense and trouble?

All this is rather sad, for she was just a social misfit, an eccentric old woman starved of kindness, dying miserably of cold and drink and mourned by no one – or was she?

A gravestone?

34
Map Ref
ST 590444

CROSCOMBE

The Seven Guilds

At the south-west end of St Mary's Church, Croscombe, with its magnificent Jacobean, dark oak, carved rood screen, the noble pulpit and the box pews, is the sixteenth-century two-storeyed Treasury. It has a stout door and all the windows are heavily barred, even though the first floor was used for purely secular purposes. It was here that the Seven Guilds of Croscombe used to meet to discuss the business of the village, from the distribution of charity to the admission of apprentices to the local trades, the principal one being the woollen trade. The Seven Guilds were The Young Men, The Maidens, The Webbers, The Fullers, The Archers, The Hogglers* and The Wives.

Although the woollen trade died out many years ago, its successor, silk, is still remembered by the local people. A few yards down the hill from the church, opposite the old stone cross, are the remains of the silk mill – a three-storeyed building with a date stone *c.* 1870, a tall old brick chimney and the even older wheel-pit for the 14ft by 5ft waterwheel.

The guilds' room window above the Treasury.

* Who exactly 'The Hogglers' were has not been resolved, opinion being divided between labourers and swine tenders.

35
Map Ref
ST 140367

CROWCOMBE

Bench Ends

Close to Georgian Crowcombe House, built in about 1725, and opposite the sixteenth-century Church House, the fourteenth-century Church of the Holy Ghost nestles under the wooded west slopes of the Quantock Hills.

The bench-ends in the church are superb examples of sixteenth-century craftsmanship, with the subject matter of three of them giving a clue to the remoteness the village once had. One depicts two naked men with clubs fighting a two-headed dragon (St Michael slaying the dragon?) amid a vine and bunches of grapes, with the other two giving rather more than a nod to the old pagan beliefs. One

is of a fearsome green man, with vines coming out of his mouth and cornucopias sprouting from his ears, holding two men fighting with clubs; this represents winter. The other is also a green man, also with vines growing from his mouth, but with a far more benign visage; he represents summer.

Above, left: The Green Man representing summer.

Above, right: The Green Man representing winter.

Right: St Michael slaying the dragon – with an assistant.

36
Map Ref
ST 376241

CURRY RIVEL

The Monument

Variously known as the Parkfield Monument, Burton Steeple or, more usually, Burton Pynsent Monument, this 150ft-high column is built on the edge of an escarpment overlooking West Sedgemoor, the Vale of Taunton Deane, the Brendons, the Quantocks and across to Wales.

Pynsent Monument, *c.* 1906. *(Mike Jones)*

William Pitt (the Elder), Lord Chatham, was opposed to a proposed tax of 10*s* on every hogshead of cider made, and spoke eloquently against the tax in Parliament. Sir William Pynsent had his estate at Burton (now known as Burton Pynsent) and would have been greatly affected by the tax. In gratitude for Pitt's efforts, and having no legitimate children to whom he could leave his estate, Sir William altered his will and named Pitt as his heir, even though the two had never met.

Sir William died in 1765 and in 1767 Pitt had this memorial erected, with a stone plaque 'Sacred to the Memory of Sir William Pynsent' and a quotation from Virgil, '*Hoc saltem fungram inani munere*' ('This, at least, has been done to reward the useless' or 'This, at least, has been enacted to give to the poor'). In both translations the meaning seems somewhat ambiguous.

The Tuscan column was designed by Capability Brown and cost £2,000, although it is thought that above the capital, the platform and the drum surmounted by an urn, was Pitt's own idea.

The monument's massive base has been an irresistible target for all those wanting to carve their initials and date – the earliest found is 1770, only three years after it was built, even though it was then surrounded by iron railings.

There is a rather pathetic footnote. Some years ago the door to the column was not secure, and a cow, for reasons of her own, made two attempts to climb the stairs; she was coaxed down but on her third attempt she climbed the 175 steps of the spiral staircase to the top of the column, where she fell off! The door is now secure and the monument only opened occasionally for charity.

Incidentally, the little stone-pillared, domed pavilion set on a low hilltop opposite Wadeford House, near Chard (ST 306105), is said to have come from Burton Pynsent.

CUTCOMBE

Bankdown Kennel

37
Map Ref
SS 881401

Codsend Moor is one of the bleakest and most elevated areas of Exmoor for it rises to the 1,706ft-high Dunkery Beacon (the highest point on Exmoor) and forms the headwaters of the River Quarme. Making a meagre living from the poor ground surrounding it must have been hard, but it is evident from the remains of the farm and cornmill at Bankdown that, in this area at least, some success was achieved. The farm had only 63 acres of enclosed ground, certainly not enough to have warranted its own mill with its expensive French

Above: The barn and stable at Bankdown.

Right: The kennel.

millstones, so Bankdown Mill must have served all the neighbouring farmsteads. The walls were solidly built of stone, to give both shelter to its people and stock against the harsh living conditions at over 900ft, and as a promise for the future. Farming must have succumbed quickly hereabouts to the country's agricultural decline before the First World War, and Bankdown's occupants departed, together with their dog. Today, ironically, the only habitable part is the stone kennel where the farm dog would have once guarded the property and stock!

DODDINGTON

A 'Modern' Kitchen Aid

The eastern end of sixteenth-century Doddington Hall was rebuilt in the early nineteenth century, when the kitchen and other offices were modernised. This included a small waterwheel in the cellar to turn the spit in the kitchen above – possibly less costly than employing a turn-spit!

The little wheel is the smallest in Somerset being 4ft in diameter but a mere 3¾in wide. Made of iron with copper buckets and shrouds (side plates) it was supplied with water through a nozzle from a 1¼in pipe; the movement to the spit above was through bevel-gears and rods, with the speed at which the spit rotated controlled from the kitchen, again by rods, to a stopcock on the pipe.

The hall is owned by the Fairfield Estate and is not open to the public. However, there is an identical wheel at the National Trust's Mottisfont Abbey in Hampshire, which was used for the same purpose.

On this side the buckets have a splash guard, which is why they cannot be seen.

40
Map Ref
SS 914278

DULVERTON

Chimneys

Built to overcome a serious down-draft problem in the fireplaces of six cottages, the chimneys stand like a line of sentinels on the south side of Jury Road in Dulverton. Would a 'stack of chimneys' be a suitable collective noun?

Chimneys in Jury Road, Dulverton.

DUNDRY

The Dole Table

Standing at 800ft on the top of the extreme northerly escarpment of the Mendip Hills, the Church of St Michael at Dundry has magnificent views over the whole of Bristol and down the valley of the Avon to the Bristol Channel, but that would have given little comfort to the poor and needy of the parish.

They would have had to rely on charity dispensed by the overseer of the parish, with the alms being handed to them over the Dole Table. This was, and is, a massive 5ft cube of dressed stone in the churchyard, just south-east of the church tower.

It seems extraordinary that all those years ago the parish went to the expense and labour of quarrying the stone, then transporting it to the village, when a far easier method of giving the alms could have been used. Perhaps the stone was there before the church was established, and might itself have some religious significance, although there is nothing similar anywhere else in the country.

The Dole Table.

42

Map Ref
ST 215406

FIDDINGTON

Sheila-na-gig

On the outside wall of St Martin of Tours Church, Fiddington, high up the south-east corner of the nave, is a rough, reddish stone quoin on which is carved a figure, now so worn that it has to be looked for. Here is a 'Sheila-na-gig' which, translated from the Irish, means 'Sheila of the Paps'.

These figures are common in Ireland but only thirty-seven have so far been found in England, the majority being in the west of the country, where the tradition was brought across the Irish Sea; there are three in Somerset, the other two being on roof bosses in the West Cloister of Wells Cathedral.

Sheila-na-gigs are usually represented as a female figure in a squatting position, with one or both hands under her thighs holding her legs apart to show her genitalia, which are generally exaggerated. Here at Fiddington, one arm is held up with the other resting on her knee. The head and upper body are well defined, but the lower trunk and thighs are less clear. Perhaps this is through weathering or because at some time an attempt was made to hide the erotic nature of the figure by chipping some of it away.

It is not clear why these figures should be on or in churches; were they fertility figures like those so often found in early Asian, South American and European cultures? Or, as is postulated, for some kind of instructional purpose, representing one of the Seven Deadly Sins, Lust, the others being Pride, Covetousness, Anger, Gluttony, Envy and Sloth.

Below, left:
Sheila-na-gig on
the wall of the
church.

Below, right:
A drawing of
the Sheila-na-
gig. *(Fiddington
Parochial Church
Council)*

FROME

The Town Bridge

Not as elegant as Pulteney Bridge in Bath, the Town Bridge at Frome is, nevertheless, a rarity in Britain, for on one side of it are

the frontages of houses built over the River Frome. There has long been a bridge over the river here and this is probably the fourth, having been built in 1821 by the County Surveyor, G.A. Underwood, to complete the new road through Frome, from the North Parade (*c.* 1797) and the construction of Bath Street in 1810. The bridge is built of stone with one elliptical arch to the south and two smaller arches on the town side. All the houses on the bridge were built to match the terraces in Bath Street with one exception, no. 3, which was rebuilt in the late nineteenth century.

Why was the unusual step taken to build houses on the bridge? One possible explanation could be that the town of Frome enjoyed an economic boom in the late eighteenth and early nineteenth centuries and houses and shop sites must have been at a premium on any level sections of that hilly town.

With the exception of Bath, the only other bridge in Britain with significant buildings across it is in Lincoln.

Above: The bridge and houses from the rear, *c.* 1917. *(David Greenfield)*

Below: The bridge with houses and shops on it.

GAWBRIDGE

A Hole in the Wall

Throughout the centuries corn mills suffered from three recurrent problems – floods, fire and the depredations of rodents, especially mice. The first two were rather out of a miller's control, but the last could be coped with, by having cats which had the free run of the mill. So that the cat could come and go at will, holes were usually cut into doors, low enough for the cats to jump through but high enough to prevent easy access for the rodents. Gawbridge Mill, or Gorebridge as it was spelt, has this unique, beautiful little cat hole built into its brick wall. One wonders how many times and how many cats came in and out of it, to so wear down its edges?

There's no cat flap!

GLASTONBURY

45
Map Ref
ST 503390

Commit No Nuisance

During the nineteenth century Glastonbury's water supply was 'modernised' by having it piped from springs above the town into a small grass-covered reservoir at the top of the High Street, from where it could be distributed to houses and water-points throughout the town. On the roadside by the reservoir was a water tap under an ornate columned canopy, and although Glastonbury's coat of arms has worn so badly as to be indistinguishable, on the apex of the canopy a finger, carved in relief, it still points 'To the Tor'.

But another notice was added, probably shortly after this water-point was installed. The canopied recess would have provided a quiet and secluded place for men to relieve themselves on returning from the town's public houses, so the council, and the police, took measures to stop this unsanitary practice. To one side, inscribed into the stonework, is the stern warning: 'Police Notice. Commit No Nuisance'.

Above: The police notice.

Below: The drinking fountain, a trapdoor into the reservoir and its grass-covered roof.

46

Map Ref
ST 494382

GLASTONBURY

The Holy Thorn

The legend of Glastonbury's Holy Thorn tells of Joseph of Arimathea, who was possibly the Virgin Mary's uncle, coming to Britain in about AD 31 with eleven disciples and visiting Glastonbury, by then one of Britain's foremost Christian settlements. He was supposed to have planted his staff on Wearyall Hill, just south of the town; it took root, sprouted and when it blossomed it did so at Christmas time as well as in the spring, thus spanning Christ's death and birth.

The common blackthorn, *Crataeges monogyna*, around which so many old superstitions and customs had grown up, would have been well known on the Somerset hills, with its clouds of white flowers in April and May looking for all the world like great banks of snow – hence 'a blackthorn winter'. The fact that the Glastonbury thorns – for many scions were taken – bloomed and bore green leaves at Christmas time, must have been a great wonder, but it is now known that a variety of blackthorn, *C. monogyna* 'Biflora', grows in the Mediterranean region, blossoming twice a year – in the winter and again in the spring – so that anyone coming from that region

The thorn on Wearyall Hill, with the Tor in the distance.

could have brought a sprig back and planted it. As any hedger knows, blackthorn is one of the easiest trees to 'strike'.

The first reference to a Holy Thorn, was in an anonymous poem written in the sixteenth century which mentions three thorn trees growing on Wearyall Hill which 'Do burge and beare green leaves at Christmas as freshe as others in May'. Joseph of Arimathea's role in bringing the thorn was not mentioned at all until the seventeenth century, long after Glastonbury Abbey was dissolved and even longer after the area's association with the Arthurian legend and the Holy Grail. The Holy Thorn then became another reason – and a profitable one for Glastonbury – for pilgrims to visit the area and take away a sprig of the thorn, to the great detriment of the thorn tree growing on Wearyall Hill, so that scions of the thorn are scattered throughout Britain. When the Gregorian calendar was introduced in 1752, thousands flocked to Glastonbury to see if the thorns would follow the season or the new calendar!

Surprisingly the blackthorn, although used for centuries as a boundary marker, is not a long-lived tree, so that many of the Holy Thorns now existing are probably scions of scions.

One comparatively new tradition has been introduced; a sprig of the thorn in St John's churchyard in Glastonbury is sent to the monarch every Christmas, and it is said that the Queen has it placed on the breakfast table on Christmas Day.

There is a footpath and a seat by the thorn on Wearyall Hill.

GOATHURST

Robin Hood's Hut

47
Map Ref
ST 251332

In the mid-eighteenth century the fashion in garden design changed, and at the forefront of that change were three friends: Henry Hoare II of Stourhead, Copplestone Warre Bampfyld of Hestercombe and Sir Charles Kemeys Tynte of Halswell Park, Goathurst. When Sir Charles inherited Halswell in 1740 he set to work on his grounds on a scale comparable to those of his friends; constructing linked ponds with a Bath-stone bridge, a Druid's temple, a stepped pyramid, a rotunda and a rock-work screen. Further away at the bottom of the hill was the Temple of Harmony, based on a design of Palladio's Quattro Libre, and high above Halswell House, sheltered by a belt of trees, Robin Hood's Hut.

Sadly, while Stourhead has been in the care of the National Trust for many years and Hestercombe has been saved, Halswell

Above: Robin Hood's Hut; *below*: the pyramidal well-head.

Park went into decline: ponds silted up, structures crumbled and objects were removed or destroyed. Changes are at last taking place, although the parkland has gone. The Temple of Harmony has been restored by the Somerset Building Preservation Trust (SBPT) and the house itself and other buildings are in the process of restoration.

Robin Hood's Hut had no connection with Robin of Locksley or Sherwood Forest but is an eighteenth-century allusion to the social liberties epitomised by Robin Hood. It was constructed in about 1760 as a building in which the family and visitors could take tea and admire the glorious vista stretching down to the Bristol Channel and distant Wales. It had three rooms: an earth-floored hermit's room, a kitchen, the china room in which to eat, and a splendid Gothic umbrello where the views could be enjoyed in the open air. The hut was thatched and the umbrello had a plasterwork frieze of trailing vines, while the dome had moulded swagged draperies.

By the 1970s it was in grave disrepair with the rain coming in through the thatch. Again the SBPT rescued it, but it needed constant care, so the Landmark Trust was approached. The Trust took the hut over, fully restored it inside and out, and it is now a holiday let. There is a public footpath nearby.

Close to Halswell House itself there is a small, 6ft-square, stepped stone pyramid with an inscription that reads 'To a dear Nymph'. This is now known to refer to a much-loved niece of Sir Charles, who died in 1741. The pyramid did, however, have a practical use as well, for it was a water-tank supplying the house, besides being a memorial. It remains in private ownership.

Temple of Harmony.

48

Map Ref
SS 867321

HAWKRIDGE

Crossing the Barle

On the direct route from Hawkridge to Winsford can be found what is probably the oldest bridge in Somerset, if not the country – Tarr Steps. As the Celtic word for causeway was 'tocha', with a slight corruption in its pronunciation sounding like 'tar', this clapper or causeway bridge was long held to be Celtic in origin. It is now thought to be medieval and a very primitive packhorse bridge dating from about 1200. Resting on rough stone piers set into the riverbed, its 180ft length consists of seventeen spans of fairly level stone slabs, some over a ton in weight. This provided an easy walkway some 3ft above the River Barle's normal level, and would have posed no problem to the sure-footed packhorses with their panniers of goods or sacks of wool. It is generally acknowledged that this causeway bridge is the finest in Britain.

Tarr Steps from the east.

Floods have damaged Tarr Steps in the past. On the last occasion the Royal Engineers had to rescue some of these massive slabs, which had been swept downstream, and then reposition them. The damage was caused by large trees coming down with the floodwater and acting as battering rams against the stones. A wire hawser has now been stretched between the banks upriver to catch any before damage can be done.

The Devil was said to have rights over the bridge, including that to sunbathe, and woe-betide anyone trying to cross. The local parson came to remonstrate with him and after much debate the Devil was persuaded to let travellers use it unhindered, although he did retain his sunbathing rights.

About 2½ miles upstream from Tarr Steps, at the end of a little lane leading east from Newhouse, just south of Withypool, the walker comes to the broad, fast-flowing River Barle. There is no bridge but the river can be crossed dry-shod, for there are stepping-stones – twenty-four of them (ST 851350). Not rounded, slippery stones but broad and flat, hewn from a quarry, each stone retaining a hole or slot so that they might be lifted into place, although it has been suggested that these holes once held an iron handrail. Unlikely, as the rails would have collected any debris when the Barle was in flood. Their age is unknown but they were possibly put there so that fishermen could easily cross between river banks.

Stepping stones just south of Withypool.

49
Map Ref
ST 433305

HIGH HAM

Stembridge Windmill

Marilyn Ewens

HIGH HAM WINDMILL

On the dry slopes of central Somerset and the flat wetlands of Sedgemoor where waterwheels were impractical, windmills were essential if corn was to be ground. At first all windmills were 'post mills', whereby the whole mill and its sails were built on a single large post, set deep in the ground, and the mill turned on this post to set the sails into the wind. Unfortunately, they were easily blown down in a strong gale, so they were gradually replaced with tower mills. The brick or stone towers, which contained all the machinery and mill stones, had a rotating 'cap', which allowed the sails to be set into the wind, either by hand or automatically with a vane.

Built in 1822, Stembridge was such a replacement, with its 26ft-high tower being built on the old mill mound, and continued to be worked by wind until 1897 when a boiler and steam engine took over, located in a building beside the tower. During this period it was worked by a well-known Somerset milling family, the Spearings. It is now owned by the National Trust which, in 1971, had its common sails replaced, when the canvas could be set by hand. Most of the machinery is complete, but what makes Stembridge Mill unique is that its cap is thatched – once a common practice with windmills, but now a very rare sight.

Today there are fifteen mill towers left in Somerset: the one at Chapel Alerton is complete, a few have been converted into unusual houses, but most are in ruins.

Above: The thatched Stembridge windmill. *Drawing by Marilyn Ewens.*

Right: Bench-end at Bishops Lydeard depicting a post mill.

HOLFORD

The Dog Pound

50
Map Ref
ST 152411

Tradition has it that this high-walled, open yard at Holford was built to impound stray dogs which came to the nearby kennels of the local

foxhounds, attracted by the smell of the carcases hanging in the woods – the only way dog meat could be kept reasonably fresh at that time. Although the high walls of the pound support this theory, any stray dogs causing this problem were more likely to have been shot by the huntsmen.

It is probable, therefore, that this was a general pound for stray animals and that the crest on the top of the front wall gave it its name – The Dog Pound. The crest, depicting the armorial bearings of a dog sitting, is that of the St Aubyn family who had lived at nearby Alfoxton House since the fifteenth century. No doubt stray hounds from neighbouring hunts could have been lodged there, for they would not have been accepted by the local hounds in their kennels. There are two slots high in the walls where anyone mounted on a horse could see in and identify their animals within the pound.

In 1982 the family of John Lancelot Brereton, a descendant of the St Aubyns, gave the pound to the village of Holford. The door is now blocked up.

The Dog Pound and crest.

51

Map Ref
ST 360146

ILMINSTER

The Stook

On the west side of the square in Ilminster is a 6ft-high, stumpy, octagonal pillar, built of Hamstone, with a flattened, cone-shaped top. It could be a bollard to prevent vehicles mounting the pavement, but it is not, although it now acts as one. It is an old conduit and it once had a spout from which flowed a constant supply of pure water, piped from a spring further up the hill. It was one of the town's main water supplies, where the inhabitants could collect drinking water in buckets and no doubt gather to exchange news and gossip. (It is now recognised as a fact that communal contact with live water is conducive to companionable talk.) It became affectionately known as the Stook from its resemblance in shape to a shock (sheaf) of corn when standing upright in a stook.

The Stook is immediately opposite the old open-sided Market House, a little gem of a building, and sits beside the former George Hotel, where the future Queen Victoria spent her first night in a hotel when she was six months old.

The Stook.

52

Map Ref
ST 344170

ILTON

A Double-decker Pillbox

When a German invasion seemed imminent in 1940, a series of defensive stop lines was built across Britain. They were based along natural and artificial obstacles such as rivers or railway lines, and were defended by concrete pillboxes and gun emplacements. One such stop line was across the waist of the west of England, from Seaton on the English Channel to the mouth of the River Parrett on the Bristol Channel. The vast majority of the pillboxes – there were over 300 built along this line alone, with some 200 still surviving – were constructed to set designs, but the one near Ilton is an exception. The railway line from Chard to Taunton (still much in use at that time) formed part of this defensive line and on this particular stretch ran along a low embankment. A pillbox was needed here so that British troops could fire over the top of the embankment at the enemy crossing the flat meadows to the west, with another to guard against a lateral advance along the line itself. To prevent one pillbox from blocking the fire of the other they were stacked up as a double-decker, unfortunately making it a very prominent and obvious structure. So it was disguised as a rail-side engine water-filling tank, with a black-painted wooden tank on the top, its sides made to look like brickwork and the embrasures covered by hessian. How effective this pillbox would have been if put to the test is problematical, but certainly the soldiers manning the upper box would have been somewhat exposed. Happily, the occasion never arose.

Above: The double-decker pillbox as it appeared in 1941. *(Somerset Records Office)*

Left: The pillbox today.

53
Map Ref
ST 335162

ILTON

The Gingerbread House

The Speke family had been the owners of a vast acreage of south Somerset for generations. However, Jordans, the last of their great houses, was demolished in the 1960s. The gardens have been left to grass over and although the high walls surrounding the old kitchen garden survive, nothing now grows there. The woodland walk is overgrown, but at the far end the little cottage in which the head gardener once lived has been lovingly restored by a descendant, Mr P. Speke, and his children aptly christened it the Gingerbread House.

It is not quite a 'cottage orné', for Somerset is not noted for these (Devon is a far happier hunting ground), but it is a quirky little cottage, typical of those built as lodges or for senior servants. It is almost circular with central chimneys and has one upper room. It is thatched, with beetling eyebrows over the windows and doors, and the thatch extending out some 4ft from the walls is supported by wooden posts. It was built in about the 1820s by the father of Captain John Hanning Speke, the famous mid-nineteenth century explorer of Africa.

The Gingerbread House.

KILMERSDON

The Ammerdown Lighthouse

54
Map Ref
ST 718521

The Ammerdown lighthouse or, to give it its correct name, the Ammerdown Park Column, was designed by Joseph Jopling and erected by Lord Hylton 'to commemorate the genius, energy and brilliant talents' of his forebear, Joseph Samuel Jolliffe, who died in 1824, for 'he was slave to no party and bigot to no sect'. What prompted Lord Hylton to build it thirty years later is as unclear as to why it was built as a near replica of the Eddystone lighthouse, for the sea is nearly 30 miles away. It is recorded that the inscription around the base – in English, French and Latin – tells of the profound affection held for Jolliffe by Lord Hylton.

The lighthouse.

When the lighthouse was built it was in the middle of rolling downland, now huge arable fields. The 150ft-high column is set on a square base with three windows and a door, from which it sweeps up to a moulded glass dome, or viewing lantern, which could be illuminated. The bottom of the stairs was lit by portholes. The four Coade stone animals which once guarded the base of the column are at Ammerdown House.

The column is now enclosed by iron railings and a veritable jungle of brambles and thorn, but it can be seen from the nearby track.

KILVE

The Somerset Oil Field

Between the car park and the sea at Kilve there stands a strange Grade II listed structure, with a plaque briefly describing it. It is a monument to a failed industry – the massive remains of an oil-refining retort.

During the nineteenth century most of Britain's limited oil requirements (then mainly lighting and lubricating oils) were imported from the USA, but in Scotland oil had been successfully extracted from oil shale since the 1850s. In 1914 similar oil shale deposits were found along the north Somerset coast and in 1920 drillings to over 1,000ft showed sulphur-free oil-bearing shale. It was estimated that in the 10 square miles prospected there was over 200 million tons of oil shale and that each ton could produce 40 gallons of oil. In 1923 two companies, the Williton Syndicate Ltd and Shaline Ltd, were formed to exploit the shale, with plant at Combwich and Kilve; their seventy-two retorts were fired with that same oil shale, producing petrol, fuel oil, paraffin and lubricating oil, plus the extracted limestone which was burnt for cement and lime. Some 500 houses were to be built as homes for the envisaged number of employees.

The oil retort,
c. 1923.
(Mike Jones)

An experimental plant was built at Kilve in 1924 (its one retort, at 35ft tall, being half the size of those in Scotland) under a John Black, who had managed an oil shale refinery in Scotland. The shale used was from open-cast workings and the oil yield was only five to ten gallons per ton and had a far too high sulphur content. This meant that the shale would have to be mined from the deeper seams and would prove disastrously uneconomic.

So ended Somerset's oil boom, but had it succeeded, how different this part of the county would look today!

LANGPORT

Swing Bridge

When the Great Western Railway's branch line to Yeovil reached Langport in 1906, it had to run between Bow Bridge and the steep little hill leading out of the town to Curry Rivel. This necessitated a road bridge over the line, and to ease the steep gradient this would

56
Map Ref
ST 414266

Swing bridge
– open.

Swing bridge
– closed.

have involved, the road was embanked from the west end of Bow Bridge, with a vertical retaining wall to the north.

There was a public house, renamed the Railway Hotel, close to this wall on the old road level, and because wagons had to go up what became a service road to warehouses behind the hotel, there was little room for access to the hotel itself. The answer was to make the hotel's main entrance on the first floor, level with the now embanked road, with a footbridge connecting the two. However, wagons could not pass under a normal footbridge, so a novel solution was built: a swing bridge, split lengthways down the middle – one half swinging west and the other half east, with neither half, when open, obstructing the service road. The hotel has now been converted into flats, with two of them retaining this unique means of entry.

In a town noted for the number of its drinking parlours, the Railway Hotel reputedly had the longest bar in Langport!

LANGPORT

The Hanging Chapel

Despite its name, the hanging chapel never had any sinister connotations but, being built over the east gate of Langport's town wall, it just hangs in the air over the roadway.

Originally a chantry chapel dating from the thirteenth century, it is first mentioned in 1344, dedicated to the blessed Virgin Mary, but was soon abandoned, thereafter having a chequered history. For many years it was the guilds' meeting room then, in 1596, it became Langport's town hall, but only for four years, before becoming the grammar school until 1790. It then became an arms store for the local militia during the Napoleonic scares, a Sunday school, the private museum of a local ornithologist, Edward Quekett, to house his collection of stuffed birds, and the lodge of a Masonic order.

It was extensively restored in the nineteenth century and has now been scheduled as an ancient monument, although not generally open to the public. To see both sides don't walk through the archway, for the traffic seldom slows down – use the little snicket on the east side.

The hanging chapel.

58

Map Ref
ST 172453

LILSTOCK

A Deserted Harbour

Where a little stream enters the sea at Lilstock on the west Somerset coast, in about 1820, Sir John Ackland of Fairfield House, Stogursey, built a boathouse close to where boats from South Wales could be beached, bringing in coal and limestone for the estate's limekilns, with pit props being exported. A few years later the doctor of Sir John's granddaughter, who was in delicate health, prescribed sea air and light exercise; so a little wooden house was built for her here and a short promenade where she could walk or drive in her carriage. It did the trick for shortly afterwards she married Sir Alexander Hood of St Audries.

At the same time the stream was diverted eastwards in a wide masonry channel between the cliff and the promenade, with a lock gate at its seaward end so that water could be pounded up to enable boats to berth at high water. This pond could also be opened quickly (when no boats were in) to allow a rush of water to clear the entrance of the channel of any pebbles which might have accumulated. By 1848 the harbour had a resident coastguard and some ten years later the amount of trade warranted a customs officer, with as many as three

Lilstock harbour from the Ordnance Survey 25in : 1 mile County Series map of 1903.

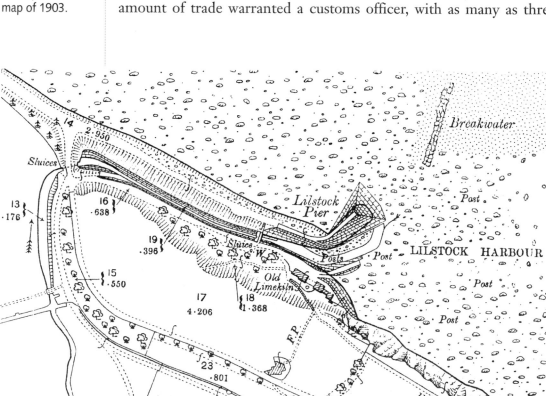

The lock gate
recess, 1978.

boats berthed at the same time. There were warehouses and in about 1860 a stone jetty was constructed to protect the harbour mouth. The promenade became a fashionable venue and a little pavilion was built, with pleasure paddle steamers calling regularly on their way between Burnham and Ilfracombe.

However, it became increasingly difficult to keep the entrance clear of pebbles, and trade declined, the final blow being the great gale of 28/29 December 1900, when the jetty was destroyed and the configuration of the beach drastically altered. Today, only the masonry of the channel with the recess for the lock gate, the foundations of a warehouse, the remains of the long, curving breakwater and the line of the promenade can be seen.

Lilstock Harbour was in many ways similar to that at Porlock Weir (SS 863480), which is still used by small pleasure craft.

The hamlet of Lilstock, which had a population of ninety-four in 1881, now consists only of a farmhouse and a couple of cottages. Its church, St Andrew's, was partly demolished with just the chancel being retained as a mortuary chapel, and the inn, the Limpet Shell, has gone, although whether this was in the hamlet or by the harbour is not known.

In his book of 1909, *The Somerset Coast*, Charles Harper, describing the harbour, wrote of 'a lonely cottage amid the elms, the end of everything, a veritable dead end. You climb to the lonely beach and have it all to yourself; the grey sea splashing amid the ooze and scattered boulders, and a great empty sky above'. It is little changed.

59

Map Ref
ST 466259

LONG SUTTON

Friends' Meeting House

The Religious Society of Friends was founded by George Fox in 1652. Its members became known as Quakers because Fox told a judge to 'tremble at the word of the lord'. Fox came to the area around Long Sutton near Somerton in 1656 and his preachings attracted many of the farming, craftsmen and shopkeeping classes, with a few professionals and labourers. Because Quaker beliefs forbade them to pay tithes to the Church, swear an oath in court or take off their hats to a judge, they suffered persecution, being unable to bury their dead in the local churchyard and having to hold their meetings in private houses or in barns. With growing religious tolerance, they became recognised and were able to build meeting houses and have their own burial grounds. The meeting house at Long Sutton was one of the first to be built and is considered to be one of the best in the country.

Friends' Meeting House, Long Sutton. Note the orderly headstones.

It was built in 1717 with a bequest from William Steele, although the members were 'at the charge of the carriage of the materials'. Queen Anne in style, it is constructed of local lias stone with Hamstone

mouldings under a slate roof, and with sash windows still with their original glazing bars and the occasional blown glass. Inside it conforms with all Friends' meeting houses – simplicity – to induce a feeling of utter calm. The walls are white and without ornamentation and the free-standing benches are of bleached elm, with one on a dais at one end. (Quakers worship in silence, facing the centre of the room, with no order of service or priest and the members speaking as the spirit moves them.) At the other end of the room is a gallery which can be closed off from the main room by solid wooden shutters which, unusually, slide up and down, where women's business was once conducted.

The burial ground is also unusual, as all the stones and inscriptions are of the same size and style – for in death all are equal – so unlike those in churchyards and cemeteries where fancy and/or money dictates the choice of monuments.

Outside the gate onto the road is a reminder of another age when, as now, members came from a wide area. There is a stone mounting-block to assist the ladies to mount their horses, for they would have ridden either side saddle or pillion behind their menfolk.

To see inside the meeting house a key can be obtained from the neighbouring house and all are welcome to meetings on Sundays.

The mounting-block by the roadside.

LOPEN

60
Map Ref
ST 427139

Romano-British Villa

Commencing at Lincoln and ending at Exeter, that great Roman road, the Fosse Way, bisects Somerset from the north-east, near Bath, to the south-west, near Ilminster. Even where present-day roads do not follow the old Fosse Way, its course can be traced by footpaths, byways and field boundaries. Because the road made so much of Somerset's rich and fertile land accessible, many villas and large farmsteads were established along its route.

Lopen is only half a mile south of the Fosse Way and in October 2001 a sharp-eyed mechanical-digger operator spotted some little cubes of coloured stone – and so was discovered the largest Romano-British villa and mosaic floor in the country. Archaeologists from Somerset and English Heritage were alerted, but it was imperative that any work should be completed before the winter set in. So with many helpers, the excavation was completed in three weeks.

The foundations of two rooms were uncovered (with a possible heating chamber), the greater part of three others and evidence of a further three, all connected to a corridor running along the north side of the building. Unfortunately, the whole site could not be excavated because much of it lay below the level of existing farm buildings.

A section of the Romano-British mosaic at Lopen depicting a dolphin. *From a painting by Angela Naunton Davies.*

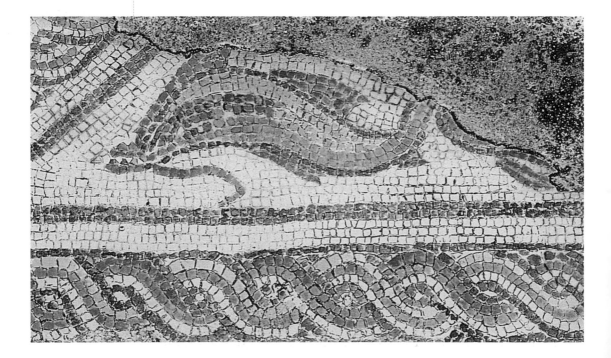

Remains of mosaic flooring were discovered in the corridor and in the other rooms, but it was the living room that revealed the largest and finest Romano-British mosaic floor, *c.* AD 360, so far found in Britain. The room is some 23ft square, with an ante-room 16ft square leading off the corridor. The ante-room was up a step from the corridor so that the view on entering this 39ft-long room would have been impressive, for in addition to the mosaic there is evidence that the walls were of painted plaster. The mosaic is thought to be the work of the Saltire School in Cirencester, with designs of large squares, St Andrew's cross, flowers, fish and canthari (two-handed drinking vessels) in various designs of blue, white, buff, brown and terracotta.

Once everything had been recorded the whole site was covered over with sand and soil to preserve it for posterity. However, a group of local people thought that there should be some tangible reminder of the villa's existence. When the site was being excavated some 6–7,000 loose pieces of tesserae and tile were uncovered, dislodged over the centuries by tree roots, building work, and so on. Enough correctly coloured pieces were assembled to reconstruct a panel of the original mosaic to depict a cantharus; these were then affixed to a slab of lias stone with a lime-based Roman cement, similar to that used by the original builders of the villa. This panel is now displayed in nearby All Saints' Church.

LOW HAM

A Dream Unfulfilled

61
Map Ref
ST 432290

The little church at Low Ham near Somerton stands forlornly in a sea of grass. No wall or hedge surrounds it, there are no gravestones, not even a made-up path leads to it; just cattle, sheep and old farm machinery nudging its walls. It was begun in 1622 by Sir Edward Hext as a chapel for his manor house and consecrated in 1669, but it never became the chapel for the grand house envisaged by his great grandson, John, 2nd Baron Stawell.

When John inherited the estate in 1682 he became the owner of twenty-eight manors, and on reaching the age of 21 he said he 'would have the finest house, the finest wife and the finest horse in Somerset' and set about realising his dream which, nearly bankrupted the family in the process. He married the daughter of Cecil, Earl of Salisbury, sold all his manors except that at Cothelstone and one in Dorset, and planned a palatial mansion. It was to be sited west of the chapel and was to be 400ft long and 100ft broad, with terraced gardens sloping

Above: The Church and garden terraces at Low Ham.

Below: Gateway at Sparkford.

gently up Hext Hill. There was to be a dovecote, a bell tower and even a canal, some 70ft by 40ft, with a waterfall from a spring. After spending £100,000 on his grand design, in 1692 he died, aged 24, leaving the mansion unfinished and to be sold off by his heirs. Today nothing remains of the house, although the terraces and other groundworks for the grand gardens can still be clearly seen.

The gateway to this dream was built and remains in existence, although not in its original location. (It is described by Pevsner as a 'segmental arch, with broad pilasters and with rudimentary Ionic capitals and broad volutes'.) In the early nineteenth century, Hazelgrove House, near Sparkford, was owned by the Mildmay family who wanted a gateway to enhance the entrance to their mile-long drive. As there was this gateway at Low Ham leading nowhere, they had it dismantled, every stone numbered and noted, loaded on to twenty wagons drawn by forty horses and taken the 10 miles to Sparkford, where it was re-erected (ST 600249) at the entrance to the drive on the main road. Alas, it no longer serves that purpose, for in the 1970s a new dual-carriage bypass to Sparkford was built, cutting through the drive and leaving the arch as a grand, though now rather pretentious, entrance leading only to the old gatehouse.

MARTOCK

Scratch or Mass Dials

62
Map Ref
ST 461191

Before the advent of clocks people lived by the rising and setting of the sun and by the church bell to call them to prayers. The priest and the bell-ringer, however, needed to know the time, for services, especially Mass, were at prescribed hours of the day. Few churches would have had a sundial at that time, so the priest would have

scratched his own on a convenient stone in the south-facing church wall, using a small, upright iron rod as a primitive gnomon. The upright rod, or style, would only have cast the correct shadow for a limited period, so for other times of the year further dials were necessary with their styles bent at various angles.

The priest would have made these dials by trial and error, first scratching a horizontal line at the equinox with the style at its centre, one end of the line representing 6 a.m., the other 6 p.m. When the

Scratch dials.

sun was thought to be at its zenith at midday, a scratch would be made where the style cast its shadow, thus creating two segments, with each segment being then divided by five equidistant scratches. Probably many experimental marks would be scratched before the priest was satisfied that he had made the dial accurately, when he would incise the final scratches more deeply – the lines seen today.

Possibly because the great ecclesiastical foundation of Glastonbury was near enough for the monks to visit, these 'scratch dials' are more common in north and east Somerset than elsewhere in the West Country. In fact, over seventy have been recorded, but the Church of All Saints at Martock is exceptional; not only are there seven of these scratch dials, all in varying degrees of erosion – two on the south porch and five on the buttresses along the south wall of the church – but three have, most unusually, their circumferences inscribed as perfect circles. One is 8in in diameter, another 6in and there is a tiny one of 2½in. There is even a short style protruding from one; normally there is only a small indentation in the stone to show where the style has been.

63
Map Ref
ST 458418

MEARE

The Fish House

The monks at Glastonbury Abbey would have required a plentiful supply of fish for their Friday repasts. The abbey had been diligent in draining vast stretches of Sedgemoor, but to meet their needs for fish throughout the year, a large pond, or meare, with a circumference of 5 miles, had been retained about 3 miles from Glastonbury. In it were 'a great abundance of Pykes, trenchards, roches and eels' and the weeds growing in it supported forty pairs of swans – a great delicacy reserved for royalty and the nobility.

Between 1322 and 1335, when Adam de Sodbury was abbot, a fish house was built on the south-west bank of the meare, to house his chief fisherman or water bailiff. Here he lived on the spacious first floor, consisting of a large hall and an ante-chamber, which were reached by an external stone staircase on the south side. The three rooms on the ground floor were used for keeping the nets, fish and eel traps, and for drying, salting and storing the fish.

After the abbey had been broken up, the meare was drained in the sixteenth and early seventeenth centuries; the fish house itself, long disused, suffered a serious fire in the nineteenth century when the roof was destroyed and much of the interior gutted.

It was reroofed by the Ministry of Works and is now in the care of English Heritage. It is freely accessible on the outside and a key can be obtained from Manor Farm, next to the church, to view the interior.

The fish house.

MELLS

Graced with Art

64

Map Ref
ST 728492

St Andrew's at Mells is a splendid example of a Somerset Perpendicular parish church, where the Horner family worshipped for many generations. Yes, the little Jack Horner of nursery rhyme fame, who pulled out the plum – the Manor of Mells – when the Glastonbury Abbey estates were broken up during the Dissolution of the Monasteries.

In the Horner Chapel is the monument to the last male of the line, Edward Horner, aged 28, who was killed at Noyelles in France in 1917. He is shown as a cavalry officer with sword and tin hat, mounted on his horse, and is the only equestrian church monument in the country. The plinth is the work of architect Sir Edwin Lutyens and the monument is by Sir Alfred Munnings, the famous painter of horses. The truly beautiful stained-glass window in the chapel's east wall is by William Nicholson, artist father of Ben Nicholson*, and depicts St Francis preaching to the birds and fishes.

At the west end of the church, under the tower on the north wall, is a superb plaster-on-wood relief of a peacock sitting on an open tomb with its tail trailing down, designed by Sir Edward Burne-Jones. It is to the memory of Laura Lyttleton, wife of Alfred Lyttleton, a cabinet minister in Lord Asquith's government. On the opposite wall is a memorial to Raymond Asquith, son of the Liberal Prime Minister; the bronze wreath is the work of Lutyens and the lettering is by Eric Gill.

Equestrian memorial to Captain Edward Horner.

On another wall is a large piece of embroidery, under glass, designed by Burne-Jones and executed by Lady Frances Horner.

In the churchyard, the stone memorial for Sir John and Lady Horner was designed by Lutyens and that of Mark Horner by Eric Gill. There are also the graves of the writer Siegfried Sassoon, Violet Bonham-Carter and Monsignor Ronald Knox, the Roman Catholic priest and scholar (the Asquiths converted to Catholicism). Lutyens also designed an avenue of clipped yews, leading the eye from the north side of the church out to the open countryside – a Gertrude Jekyll influence perhaps?

The village too has been included, for the war memorial and, in the centre of the village near the river, a small triangular, open-sided stone-roofed shelter, are both designed by Lutyens.

A veritable feast of late nineteenth- and early twentieth-century art.

* Ben Nicholson became a celebrated abstract artist (1894–1982).

MIDFORD

Midford Castle

Somerset is not well blessed with castles: Dunster (National Trust), perched on top of its hill, is the most impressive and well preserved; Nunney, moated but open to the skies, is maintained in its ruinous state by English Heritage; Stogursey, also moated, has been carefully restored by the Landmark Trust as a holiday let, while bits of Taunton Castle are recognisable for what they once were.

Midford Castle, however, although castellated, is not a castle at all but a most unusual small country house, built in 1775 by Henry Woolhouse Disney Roebuck, possibly to a design by John Carter. It is trefoil in plan, three-storeyed with ogee-headed windows, battlements all around the top and an imposing turreted main entrance. Because it is built on a steep slope, the terrace, at ground level to the north, becomes about 15ft above the ground to the south, underneath which were built the coach houses and stables and, between this part of the terrace and the lower, sub-floor of the castle, is an area bridged by the main entrance. The castle commands magnificent views across the valley down to the Midford Brook and the woods of Limpley Stoke, so when seen from below, it looks every bit a true castle nestling in its wooded surroundings.

The Ace of Clubs.

Because of its trefoil shape it is known as the Ace of Clubs and thereby hangs a tale. It is said that Roebuck, a notorious gambler in the great era of gambling, staked all he had on the single turn of a card – the ace of clubs. He won, and with the £100,000 proceeds built himself a house in the shape of the ace of clubs!

It is not accessible to the public but can be clearly seen from the roads below it in the valley.

MINEHEAD

The Hobby-horse

66
Map Ref
SS 9746

It is only at Padstow in Cornwall and Minehead in Somerset that the May Day hobby-horse tradition survives in Britain. Each is vastly different from the other, with fierce debate as to which is the older. However, no mention is made of either until about 200 years ago, probably because by that time this ancient custom had become so unusual as to warrant mentioning.

The Minehead hobby-horse is known as the sailor's horse, possibly because of its shape, for the light wooden framework is built rather like a keel-up, flat-bottomed boat with pointed ends or prows. This is covered by long coloured ribbons over a base of sacking, which is decorated with brightly painted spots, each with a concentric circle of a different colour. The horse is carried on a man's shoulders, his head protruding through a hole in the top, with two holes in the sides through which he can put his hands. The man wears a grotesque mask, painted white with red embellishments, surmounted by a tall conical hat decorated with ribbons and with a tuft of feathers at the top. The horse has a pointed head and a rope tail (this was formerly a cow's tail).

The ceremonies commence on May Day morning with the beating of a large drum before the horse emerges from its secret stable near

The hobby-horse and attendants, *c.* 1930.
(Hilary Binding)

Minehead quay. Accompanied by the drum and an accordion playing 'The Minehead Tune' (which is based on a very old traditional air 'The Soldier's Joy'), the horse is paraded westwards through the town to a crossroads known as White Cross. All along the route the horse prances, pirouettes, leaps and makes obeisance to any likely-looking contributor (money was and still is the object of the exercise!). After the money is taken in through the holes in the side, the giver is then ceremoniously given a low bow. Non-givers, however, are rushed at, with the horse swinging around to try and catch the unwary with its swinging tail.

The whole performance is repeated on the evening of 3 May, only this time proceeding eastward to another crossroads known as Cher, after which the horse returns to its stable for another year. This event was once much rowdier and far more menacing, with houses being entered and demands for money made, but today it is charities which benefit.

Because there are no written records, the origin of the Minehead hobby-horse is obscure; hobby-horses are alluded to in medieval times and even Shakespeare mentions one: 'For O, for O, the hobby-horse is forgot'. So in one form or another they probably go back to antiquity and being always connected with May Day were probably fertility rites associated with the coming of spring.

But the origins of the Minehead sailor's horse could well stem from a dimly remembered folk memory relating to the repulsing of a Danish landing party by locals riding along the coast on bedecked ponies and themselves grotesquely dressed.

MONKSILVER

67
Map Ref
ST 075366

Drake's Cannon Ball

In 1582 Elizabeth Sydenham, a ravishing beauty aged 17 (there is a portrait of her in the National Maritime Museum at Greenwich), was deeply in love with Francis Drake (1540–96), who was yet to be knighted. They were to be married, but Drake went off on one of his foraging expeditions, leaving Elizabeth at her home, Combe Sydenham, near Monksilver. Elizabeth's father, Sir George Sydenham, was not in favour of the marriage, considering Drake to be little more than a pirate, and unsuitable to marry into an old family such as his. When, after three years, Drake had not returned, Sir George put pressure on Elizabeth to marry a member of another old family, the Wyndhams, who were close neighbours at Orchard

Wyndham. The marriage was arranged to take place at St Mary's in Stogumber, but as the bride-to-be was approaching the church there was a violent clap of thunder and a large meteorite crashed through its roof.

Elizabeth was quick to take this as an omen to stop the wedding and the legend grew up that it was a cannon ball fired by Drake as a warning. In fact, Drake had that very day landed at Plymouth, and hearing what was afoot, made post-haste for Combe Sydenham. Later that year he and Elizabeth were married in All Saints' Church, Monksilver. On the marriage, Drake came into possession of Buckland Abbey, in Devon, and here they lived happily until Drake died in 1596. As the poet Charles Fitz-geffrey put it at the time:

> Divorced by death, but wedded still by love
> For love by death can never be divorced.

The 'cannon ball is 14in in diameter, although not quite spherical, and weighs approximately 1cwt, and is possibly one of the largest iron meteorites ever to have fallen on this country. Over the centuries it attained its high polish by being rolled, for sport, down the nearby steep fields. A superstition grew up that ill luck would befall anyone taking it away from Combe Sydenham and it has only once been removed – with dire results to the offender.

The Hall at Combe Sydenham is in private hands but is occasionally opened to the public.

Drake's cannon ball.

MOORLINCH

Swayne's Leaps

In 1685 Jan Swayne, a farm labourer and noted wrestler of Moorlinch, threw in his lot with the Duke of Monmouth. After Monmouth's defeat at Sedgemoor on 6 July, Jan was captured, taken to Bridgwater, tried and sentenced to be hanged. In company with others he was marched along the road to Glastonbury over the Polden Hills, with his fellow prisoners being hanged, one by one, at the crossroads nearest their native village, until at last it was Jan's turn.

By chance he knew one of his captors, John Marsh, with whom he had wrestled in the past; Marsh suggested to his officer that it would be good sport to have a final wrestle before Swayne was hanged. He also suggested that Swayne should show off his prowess at jumping before the contest, so the party repaired to a grassy glade in Whitley Wood, Marsh wagering that Swayne couldn't jump 20ft.

A wink was as good as a nod, for after Jan was freed from his bonds, his first leap took him 14ft 2in, his second 12ft 10in and his third 15ft 3in – and he was into the trees and away!

After things quietened down Jan returned to his wife and children at Moorlinch, his achievement no doubt giving much amusement to

Swayne's three leaps in Whitley Wood.

all those involved in the rebellion. Over the years Jan's leaps became exaggerated, for one report gives them as 22, 20 and 18ft respectively – a feat which today would put him into the Olympics.

His astonishing leaps to freedom were recorded with stones set into the ground (*see also* entry 98) and in the nineteenth century these were replaced by small, rounded and dressed 'tombstones' (8in × 5in × 9in high) set at the relevant distances, where they can be seen today, although almost buried in leaves. They are quite close to the road (A39) and a signpost points to them along a public footpath through the wood. But be careful – the traffic along the A39 is both fast and furious and the verges are almost non-existent.

MUCHELNEY

Angels on High

69
Map Ref
ST 428249

The church of St Peter and St Paul at Muchelney was never home to the ecclesiastical life of the great Benedictine abbey which so closely adjoined it, for it was outside the abbey precincts and was used only by the local worshippers and the abbey's less distinguished visitors. The fabric of the church is, therefore, not as elaborate as one would have expected from its proximity to the abbey, but after the latter's dissolution in about 1536, one embellishment was added in the early seventeenth century.

One of the angels depicted at Muchelney.

The barrel ceiling in the nave was painted, artist unknown, with ten blue panels, each showing an angel floating above clouds; they are somewhat crudely executed but are colourful and great fun. Pevsner described them as 'lovable but incompetent'.

Incompetent they may be, but they are also unique in the depiction of angels. They are dressed in the costumes of the time but, to say the least, their décolletage is daring, with many completely and startlingly bare-breasted. Did the male worshippers of old cast their eyes down when in prayer or did they look upwards to the vision of those delights which one day awaited them?

NETHER STOWEY

Queen Jane

Opposite the road turning south off Castle Street in Nether Stowey, which eventually leads to Broomfield and Taunton, Ivy Cottage stands back from the street behind its small front garden. In the garden's west wall an arched, brick alcove frames an eye-catching, brilliantly painted, half life-sized statue of a lady in flowing robes. At first sight it could have a religious context, but this is a beautifully modelled figure of Jane Seymour, King Henry VIII's third wife. It is said that she was the only one of his wives whom he truly loved, and was distraught by her death from puerperal fever on 24 October 1537. But why commemorate her here?

The man who created this village landmark in 1970, Doug Forsey, a former Birmingham jeweller, says 'it was to fill an empty space where a doorway had been blocked up'. It was his first and only piece of sculpture, and 'was made on an old door from chicken wire and cement'.

Queen Jane.

But what a creation! She is depicted in a French-style head-dress, which suggests that she is shown as a lady-in-waiting to the previous queen, Anne Boleyn, who favoured that style.

The only connection the Seymour family had with the area was that a year after Jane's death her brother, Edward, bought the manor and estate of Nether Stowey.

NETHER STOWEY

Walford's Gibbet

The old Gibbet Oak still stands and, rather surprisingly considering that hangings were not unusual during the eighteenth century, the name survives locally and on the maps. Perhaps it was the tragic circumstances surrounding one event or because it was recorded in detail by a local man, Tom Poole, a friend of the Wordsworths when they lived at Alfoxden near Nether Stowey. In fact, William Wordsworth (1770–1859) wrote a poem about the event but it was never published, being considered too tragic a subject.

The Gibbet Oak.

John Walford was a good-looking young charcoal-burner from Nether Stowey, betrothed to Ann Rice, a miller's daughter; the betrothal was, however, broken up by the malicious tongue of John's stepmother. Because of his work tending the char heaps, John had to spend many nights in the woods, and here he was visited by 'a poor, slaternly girl' who, taking advantage of his distress, 'consoled' him. She became pregnant and John was obliged to marry her and maintain the child. At first they appeared happy, but John soon realised what a ghastly mistake he had made and rows developed. One night, going down to the local inn, the Castle of Comfort, they had a terrible row and John dealt her a violent blow which, to his utter dismay, killed her.

The next day he gave himself up to the Justices and was tried for murder at Bridgwater. Despite pleading that his action was not premeditated, he was sentenced to be hanged and, as was usual then, the sentence was to be carried out at the scene of the crime. Before a large, silent crowd, John, already bound with a rope around his neck and standing on a board across the back of a cart, asked to speak to Ann Rice if she was there. She came from the back of the crowd and they spoke for ten minutes, only being parted when he attempted to kiss her, although he did succeed in kissing her hand. He then joined in the Lord's Prayer and the Belief before saying in a strong voice 'I am guilty of the crime I am going to die for, but I did it without fore-intending it and I hope God and the world have forgiven me.' Then he opened his hand to let drop a handkerchief, the signal for the cart to go forward. The *Bristol & Bath Magazine* of 1797 reported: 'After hanging the usual time the body was taken down, placed in an iron cage and suspended from the gibbet.' It was a common saying that Walford looked better hanged than most men alive! After a year to the day that the crime was committed the body was buried 10ft deep under the oak tree.

NORTH CADBURY

The Risen and the Fallen

In the 1980s many of the sacred ornaments in the sanctuary and on the reredos in St Michael's Church, North Cadbury, were damaged beyond repair by a deranged man who broke into the church. The Parochial Church Council had to decide what, if any, replacements could be made, with the general consensus being that they should be in a modern style. A nationally known sculptor, John Richardson, who lived in the next village, Galhampton, was approached and asked to submit designs.

What he came up with was beautiful: Christ suspended, but not on a cross, with a young naked couple reaching up to him for redemption, with a similar couple falling away from him in sin. Opinions on the sculpture were, however, divided, some thinking the naturalness of the two couples unsuitable for inside the church. So a compromise was reached; the group would be placed on the east wall of the churchyard, on the high blank wall of Cadbury Court's coach house.

The group on the churchyard wall with Christ depicted in the centre.

There they hung in glory until a few years ago, when they were stolen and never recovered. Luckily, the sculptor had kept the original designs and models, so duplicates were cast and rehung in their original position, only now more securely fixed.

These must be the most unusual and bravest modern sculptures to be found in any village churchyard.

Above: The Risen and the Fallen.

NORTH CURRY

The Reeve's Feast

The reeve* for North Curry was granted a charter by King John (1199–1216) for a feast to be held yearly two days before Christmas, unless one of the feast days should fall on a Sunday. The conditions

73
Map Ref
ST 319246

* Reeve: the old English title for a steward or magistrate responsible for one or more territorial areas.

and manner of the feast are set out in writing on the wall in St Peter's and St Paul's Church, North Curry.

The reeve had to pay £4 5*s* towards the feast and the manors and tenements had to contribute three fat heifers, a pig, thirty-six bushels of wheat and £2 8*s*, but they, of course, participated in the feast. The reeve was assisted by 'Dealers' who were given a breakfast 'of two loaves of bread, 8 pennyworth of Top But of Beef, three marrow bones boiled with the marrow taken out and spread on toasted bread' and a feast each of '8 pennyworth of Beef and two pence in money and one pound of suet sent to their homes for their trouble'.

The Reeve's Feast itself is something else again, with principal guests being the 'Jacks of Knapp and Slough' (lords of the manors of Knapp and Slough, hamlets adjoining North Curry). The Jacks and the Dealers then sat down to dinner, after which 'two candles weighing a pound each lighted and until they had burnt out the two Jacks and their attendants have a right to sit drinking after dinner', with toasts to 'the Imortal Memory of King John, the Real Jack of Knapp and the Real Jack of Slough'. The reeve has to sing:

> King John he was a Noble Knight
> I am come to demand my right
> Open the door and let me in
> Else I'll carry away my money again.

The dinner consisted of 'Chine of Beef roasted and the Rump and Round boiled, the Belly piece of the forequarters of the half of pig rolled up made into a collar of brawn with a sprig of rosemary and dusted with flour. A hen with the head and tail on, the rest of the feathers except the tail plucked off, a little boiled and served upon sops of bread, proper vegetables, and a large mince pie with an effigy of King John, properly painted to represent the King, stuck up in the middle of it. Bread and ale and bread and cheese after.' The remains of the meal were to be given to the 'second poor' (those not quite destitute) and after drinking as much as they liked the Dealers received 1*s* each for holding the stirrups of the Jacks, to make sure they didn't fall off their horses going home!

The feast as described was eventually done away with because it had become something of an orgy, but did continue in a rather more sedate form until 1930. Since the Second World War, however, the feast has been revived, although it is now held only every seven years.

ORCHARDLEIGH

The Moated Church

74
Map Ref
ST 771509

Although much of the fabric of St Mary's at Orchardleigh is fourteenth century, it is an unpretentious little church with no tower or steeple, only a belfry. It is the most unusual and certainly the most secret of churches in its location and in the extreme difficulty one has in finding it. It is not signposted, the approach is through a golf course, then down an unmade and potholed track – and nowhere near the new Orchardleigh House.

St Mary's and its churchyard is set on a little island at the west end of the smaller of two lakes, and can only be approached over a narrow bridge, so perhaps moated is a better description; in any case, it is surrounded by water (and ducks) and there is no other like it in the country.

A view over the lake at Orchardleigh on a misty morning'.

The former Orchardleigh House was once close by, which explains why it is where it is; but was it always on an island, for the lake is artificial with massive dams? Perhaps it was on dry land and the lake cunningly formed around the church when the park was landscaped. The new Orchardleigh House is some half a mile away, and is now used, with the church, as a modern venue for weddings.

Erected near the south door of St Mary's is a 5ft-high stone pedestal and urn commemorating Azor, the faithful dog of Sir Thomas Champney, which died in 1796. The story of Azor being buried with Sir Thomas and the dog's subsequent 'supposed removal' from consecrated ground on the orders of the Bishop of Bath and Wells, is related with a deal of poetic licence in Sir Henry Newbolt's (1862–1938) seventeen-verse poem, 'Fidele's Grassy Tomb', from which a few lines follow:

He looked on the lake, sunny and still:
The last of earth that his eyes would see
Was the island Church of Orchardleigh.

But the last that his heart could understand
Was the touch of the tongue that licked his hand.
'Bury the dog at my feet' he said,
Before his voice stilled, and the Squire was dead.

Above: Azor's memorial.

Right: Church, bridge and moat.

PAWLETT

The Hangar

75
Map Ref
ST 284429

Where the Pawlett Hams – a lush flood plain east of the River Parrett – meets the gently rising slope up to Pawlett village, is a monstrous building completely out of place with its surroundings and seemingly there by accident.

A rusting hangar, for that is what it is, of such a size (100ft × 70ft × 80ft high) would be more suitable for an airship than for any aircraft in operation when it was put up in 1940–1 and with the nearest airfield over 10 miles away. The only comparable existing building is at Cardington which was built for airships, and the Pawlett hangar was constructed by the same company.

The balloon hangar.

Just before the Second World War the Royal Aircraft Establishment, in conjunction with the Washington Singer Laboratory at the University of Exeter, were testing the comparative strengths of British and German barrage balloon cables and how they could be cut by aircraft, using an extra-large barrage-type balloon. The operation was sited in a chalk pit (to be out of the wind) near Mildenhall in Suffolk. However, when the war came this proved unsuitable and the experiments were moved west. They went first to the Steart flats near the mouth of the Parrett, but that proved too windy, so they moved into a field surrounded by trees near Pawlett, where the experiments were continued in the open until the hangar was built.

A hangar of that size was needed so that the balloon need not be deflated each night (a mixture of air and hydrogen was used, but hydrogen, made at Weston-super-Mare gas works, was expensive); the balloon was attached to a winch on a lorry and could be trundled out each day. This was then anchored down and the balloon flown at about 500–600ft. The aircraft used to try to cut cables (suspended from the balloon and kept at a distance from the balloon cable itself by drogue parachutes) were pairs of Fairey Battles, the wings of which had specially strengthened leading edges. It was a hazardous operation, which is why two flew together – one cutting and the other with a photographer to record the results. There was also a platform on the roof of the hangar for a tripod-mounted camera reached by outside steps. The other aircraft used were Wellingtons, but these had a series of 'V' cutters on the wing edges. It was extraordinary that, for such a large aircraft to fly deliberately into a cable and at such a low height, only one was brought down, with no one killed. A Fairey Battle which crashed killed its middle-aged and then world famous photographer. One balloon did escape, was chased and eventually caught in Wiltshire – with difficulty, as there was a massive charge of static electricity in the cable until it was earthed.

The experimental work continued at Pawlett until 1944, for on the Hams was a 15ft-tall, pyramidal brick structure used as a target for the low-level dropping of 1,000lb bombs and the spread pattern of clusters of incendiary bombs, tested before the raid on Dresden. Of course, none were live and they had indicators so they could be found and recorded.

Today the future of the hangar is uncertain as it is in a very dilapidated condition, but it is the only one of its kind left except for the one at Cardington. The target was demolished in about 2000. One of the original crew at Mildenhall, Tom Flook, came to Pawlett, married, and is still there at the age of 90.

PEN HILL

Romulus and Remus

When Mars, the god of war, fathered twin sons by the vestal virgin Rhea Silvia, Amulius, the king of that region, fearful of his position, had the two babes placed in a wooden trough and cast adrift on the River Tiber. The trough drifted ashore and was found by a she-wolf who suckled them, fed them and protected them for many years, until eventually they were found by a shepherd, Faustulus, and his wife, who took in the two little boys and reared them until they were adults. When Amulius died both boys wanted the throne and a violent dispute arose, ending in Romulus killing Remus. Romulus became king and ruled the city he founded in 753 BC for forty years. That city was Rome.

An Italian POW's 'thank you'.

But what, one might ask, has all this to do with Somerset? On the east side of the Wells to Bristol road (A39) where it levels out at Pen Hill after the steep climb out of Wells, there are two ornate columns, on the top of which stands a statue of the wolf suckling the two infants. Surprisingly, this is only about sixty years old. During the Second World War there was a prisoner-of-war camp for Italians near there, but as the war continued these prisoners were allowed out to work on neighbouring farms and even to live on them as one of the family. As a gesture of goodwill for all the kindnesses so many of the prisoners had received, one of their number, a sculptor named Gaeltano Celestra, fashioned this statue and erected it where all could see this 'thank you' to the local population.

PORLOCK

Give and Take a Spire or Two

The Devil, taking a quiet stroll along the north Somerset coast, came round a headland and saw a church spire, that of St Dubricus at Porlock, a couple of miles away. He did not like churches of any kind but ones with a spire he particularly abhorred, so he tore a large rock from the cliff and threw it at the offending church (to this day the headland is called Hurlstone Point on the maps (SS 898492)). The rock missed the body of the church but knocked off the top of the spire as can be seen by its truncated shape today.

The tiny church of St Culbone, tucked away in the woods near the sea some 3 miles away, had neither tower nor belfry. For-tunately, the force of the rock hitting the spire of St Dubricus made the top piece fly off as far as Culbone, where it crashed upright on the roof of St Culbone, so giving it a tiny spire!

The official version of this story is that St Dubricus was struck by lightning and the top of the spire never replaced, while later, in the nineteenth century, the little church of St Culbone had the tiny spire built on to it. One can believe what one likes, but are the size and state of the two spires a mere coincidence?

Above: The church of St Culbone.

Left: The church of St Dubricus at Porlock.

PORTBURY

A Standing Stone

78
Map Ref
ST 502754

Opposite the lychgate to St Michael's Church on the northern outskirts of Portbury, is a menhir which originally stood in a field to the north-east of the church. In the early 1950s it was buried in an old dew pond – the reason is not recorded. In 1987 the Portbury History Society rescued it and had it re-erected on its present site.

The stone, a dolomite conglomerate of a reddish colour, would most likely have originated in about 1000 BC, near Conygar Hill. Although its purpose is unknown, it was in all probability connected with the hill fort (ST 498751), the earthworks of which overlook the village.

It is not uncommon for a Christian church to be founded near a pagan sacred place, but it is most unusual for a pagan symbol to be put up near a church – almost in its churchyard. St Michael's is an extremely old foundation, as the surviving massive yew tree in the churchyard testifies; over a 1,000 years old and, although now hollow, still has a single 20ft-high trunk. Its twin has succumbed to age and only the stump remains.

The stone by the lychgate.

79

Map Ref
ST 619482

SHEPTON MALLET

The Shambles

Although the term 'Shambles' was derived from the Latin word *scamellum*, meaning literally a bench, it became applied to slaughter-houses or, more particularly, the stalls where butchers laid out their meat for sale. However, 'Shambles' was then adopted as a general term for any stalls where farmers and smallholders came to sell their cheeses, butter, chicken, eggs and vegetables and, of course, fish. These open, pantiled stalls were set up in and around most fourteenth- and fifteenth-century market-places in country towns. In some towns, notably Totnes, Kingsbridge and Dartmouth in Devon, the stalls were in open-fronted and colonnaded buildings, or could be set up in open market houses such as the one at Ilminster; even as late as the 1930s the columned entrance to Chard's old Corn Exchange was known as the Shambles and used by a greengrocer.

As the stalls in a shambles were made of wood and therefore of a temporary nature, when open markets declined and shops became fashionable, most were cleared away. The one at Shepton Mallet is a rare survivor, and has been renovated and preserved by a far-sighted Town Council. Only one other survives in the West Country, and that is a single pantiled butcher's stall in the square at Uffculme in Devon, where its life has been extended by being converted into a seated bus-shelter.

The Shambles
with the market
cross behind.

SIMONSBATH

Pinkery Pond

Except in the valleys, there were few trees in the Forest of Exmoor, and it would now look much as it did 200 years ago had it not been for the efforts of John Knight, who bought the 20,000-acre estate from the Crown in 1818, assisted later by his son, Frederick. They built roads, planted miles of beech hedges for windbreaks, put up farmsteads and improved the land around them. They proposed a railway to take iron ore from their mines, via an inclined plane, down to Porlock Weir, and even started the earthworks before finding out that the ore in that vicinity was uneconomic to mine; but the cuttings and embankments for the railway can still be seen on the high moor.

However, their most impressive piece of work, for which no explanation has ever been discovered, is a huge pond constructed 900ft high up on the Chains, a wild and isolated area of the moor. Some 200 Irish labourers were employed building an earth dam to contain the headwaters of the River Barle to form a reservoir 7 acres in extent and 30ft deep. However, it wasn't allowed to attain that size, for the earth dam was not thought strong enough, so Pinkery Pond stays now at about 3 acres. A little below the proposed water level of the reservoir, but never connected to it, is a canal, also cut by those Irish navvies. Again, its purpose is not known, for the Knights could never have made full use of the reservoir. Was it to provide irrigation

Pinkery Pond,
c. 1912.
(Mike Jones)

The plughole found in 1912.
(Mike Jones)

water for the farms around Simonsbath, in which direction it ran –
unlikely considering the high rainfall in that area – or was it to supply
water for a water-balance on the proposed railway incline down to
Porlock Weir? Possibly some researcher in the future will find the
answers. It has been emptied once, in December 1912, when it was
drained in the fruitless search for a missing man, a Mr Stenner.

SOMERSET

81

Epitaphs

Dire warnings, pathos, humour and a little history are to be found on tombs and gravestones all over the country, but a few in Somerset have stayed in the mind.

During the rebuilding of St Mary's Church (ST 268133) at Buckland St Mary in April 1868, John Hill was fetching a wagonload of stone from Ham Hill when, coming down the steep hill from the quarry, the wagon on which he was riding overturned, crushing him to death. The inscription on his gravestone concludes, not with a moral warning but an eminently practical one: 'May all carters who read this take warning and never get on their wagon'.

Although East Coker is best known for the poem by T.S. Eliot, it does, however, have a famous son, William Dampier (1651–1715), and a brass tablet on the wall of St Michael's Church (ST 538121) celebrates his life.

> Buccaneer, Explorer, Hydrographer
> Thrice he circumnavigated the Globe and, first of all
> Englishmen, explored and described the coast of Australia.
> An exact observer of all things on Earth, Sea and Air, he
> recorded the knowledge won by years of danger and hardship
> in 'Books of Voyages' and 'A Discourse on Winds, Tides and
> Currents' which Nelson bade his Midshipmen to study and
> Humbolt praised for Scientific worth.

He died in London and lies buried in an unknown grave.

In the churchyard of St Andrew's at Old Cleeve (ST 040419) a stone commemorates the death in 1808 of a blacksmith, George Jones. During this period this particular epitaph was very popular with blacksmiths and can be seen all over the country.

> My sledge and hammer lie reclined
> My bellows too have lost their wind;
> My fire's extinct, my forge decayed
> And in the dust my vice is laid:
> My coal is spent, my iron's gone,
> My nails are driven. My work is done.

This inscription on a stone in the churchyard of St Laurence at Lydeard St Laurence (ST 127321) says it all:

> Beneath this stone in sound repose
> Lies William Rich of Lydeard close;
> Eight wives had he yet none survive
> An likewise children nine times five.
> From whom an issue vast did pour
> Of great grandchildren, five times four.
> He lived and died immensely poor.
> July the 10th aged ninety four.

John Locke (1632–1704) the great philosopher, was a close friend of the Clarke family at Chipley Court and when he died Edward Clarke had a slate memorial placed in All Saints' Church, Nynehead (ST 138226). These sweet lines are believed to be by Locke himself.

> A little book and taper's light
> Did solace me in my last night.
> My taper spent, book closed I late,
> In bed theron to meditate.
> With what improvement I think I know
> Then volumes more or sunne can show.

Probably the most miserable sentiments expressed used to be on the tomb of William Leecox in St Andrew's churchyard at Mells (they are now too worn to be read, ST 728492):

> All my inward friends uphorred me and they whom I loved are turned against me.
> My kinsfolk have failed me and my familiar friends forgotten me.
> William Leecox husband of Rachell Leecox who departed April ye 16 1700.

The last word, however, must go to John Hippersley on his tomb in St Mary's Church at Ston Easton (ST 623530):

> Reader prepare, and be not vext
> To think your turn may be the next.

SOMERSET

82

Prospect Towers

There is a fine distinction between a folly and a prospect tower. A folly is an eccentric construction to be seen and commented upon as an object of curiosity or amusement, but seldom has any practical use. A prospect tower, on the other hand, although its architecture can sometimes be eccentric, has a very practical use – it is to climb and then view the landscape from the top. Somerset has few follies but it does have its fair share of prospect towers.

When Lady Hillsborough, the only daughter of Lord Stawell of Cothelstone Manor, built her tower, in about 1780, on Cothelstone Hill (ST 189328) on the Quantocks, she may have read and been influenced by Thomson's verse 'The Seasons' (James Thomson 1700–48):

> Heav'ns what a goodly prospect spreads around
> Of hills, and dales, and woods, and lawns, and spires.
> A gaily chequered, heart expanding view
> Far as the circling eye can shoot around.

She would not have been alone, for all over the country many landowners built towers from which to view the 'prospect' or to gaze out proudly over their rolling acres. By contemporary standards Lady Hillsborough's simple ragstone tower was small – only 30ft high and

Left to right:
Towers at Cothelstone, *c.* 1908, Conygar and Willet.

15 ft across – but situated where it was it commanded spectacular views over central Somerset. Sadly, the little tower collapsed in 1917 and today is only a grassy mound, but the view is largely the same.

Conygar Tower (SS 992441) was built by Henry Fownes Luttrell in 1775 on the bare Cony Garden Hill, both to enable him to look out over the Bristol Channel and to be seen, and enhance the view, from his home, Dunster Castle. This round, 40ft-high, crenellated tower cost Luttrell rather more than he anticipated – £132 6s ½d – so he never built the two others he had planned, on Withycombe Hill and Dunkery Beacon. He also had a bill for £4 2s 6d for the cider drunk by the workmen! The tower is now in the hands of the National Trust.

Willet Tower, *c.* 1770 (ST 095335), is perched on the end of the Brendon Hills overlooking the Quantocks and is more romantic. It was made to resemble an old ruined church, with empty Gothic doors and windows, false castellations and a ruinous curtain wall. Inside, there were only wooden stairs and a wooden viewing platform. It was also romantic in another sense, for one story has it that it was built for a lady living at Willet so she 'could spend her time contemplating the view' or perhaps awaiting her lover! For the past fifty years this little tower has kept lonely company as a lookout platform of the Royal Observer Corps, with quite a different view in mind. Did those observers think of another of Thomson's poems – 'Rule Britannia'?

Winter's or Combe Tower (ST 135312), near Combe Florey, was built in 1791 and is neither beautiful nor romantic. This 50ft-high square tower had five storeys, Mr Winter living in the first three with the top two being empty shams. Did Mr Winter have pretensions of grandeur or did he just want to keep an eye on his estate? All five storeys have now been restored to make a most unusual home.

Winter's Tower near Combe Florey.

Nothing remains of the Norman castle on the top of St Michael's Hill at Montacute, for in all probability it only had palisaded earth banks, similar to that at Castle Neroche (ST 273157) near Staple Fitzpaine. It was built by William the Conqueror's brother, Robert of Mortain, to control the area, for it 'looked down like a vultures' nest upon the hills and rich valleys at its foot'. What looks down today on the magnificent Montacute House is St Michael's Tower: about 40ft high it is circular, curving in at the top to a flat roof with railings where there was once a flagpole. Over the doorway is an inscription in Greek,

'God, master of all', 'P' (possibly standing for the Phelips family) and the date, 1760; then 'Look around!'. Inside, the fifty-two steps lead up to a small round room with barred windows and a little door, which once gave access to the railed stone projections (steps) leading up to the roof. One authority states that on a clear day eighty churches can be seen. It is owned by the National Trust and is always open for the public to climb as far as the room at the top.

Only a pile of bramble-covered rubble shows where Lax's Tower (ST 564466) once stood on the 400ft-high Knapp Hill, near Wells, for it was blown up in about 1965 when it was deemed 'a danger to children'. But who built it is not clear; the Revd Robert Gilling Lax so that he 'Could look over his land and overlook his neighbours'? Or, more likely, by his son George (1769–1854) who intended to build his new home there but, finding that this would be more expensive than first thought, only constructed the tower with the materials already carted up, building his new house, Knapphill Farm, lower down the hill. George Lax was an officer in the Volunteers in 1810, ready to repel Napoleon, and later became the Mayor of Wells, remembered by a brass plate in the floor of the nave in the cathedral.

Cranmore Tower (ST 677450) is quite spectacular for it is on a 700ft hill and rises above the woods by which it is now surrounded. It was erected by Thomas Wyatt in 1863–5 for the owner, John Moore Paget, in an Italianate style, with balconies at 50 and 80ft, and with its pyramidal roof making it over 100ft high. In the late nineteenth century it needed extensive repairs because of poor foundations, but was sound enough to be used by the Home Guard and the Royal Corps of Signals during the Second World War. In 1960 it again became unsafe but was repaired by the then owner in 1980 before becoming a restaurant.

Above: St Michael's Tower at Montacute.

Below: Cranmore Tower, c. 1930. *(Mike Jones)*

The only known
photograph of
the Red Tower,
c. 1955.
(R.N. Green)

Not a trace remains of the little round tower at Red Hill (ST 414318) near Curry Rivel, which was, indeed, little: it was only 15ft high and 10ft in diameter, had one room with two small round windows, a fireplace and steps leading up to a brick-walled viewing area. The last – and smallest – of Somerset's towers, it was built by Dr Darlington of Curry Rivel in about 1910, and gave panoramic views over West Sedgemoor and across to the Quantock Hills and Bridgwater. In 1947 Dr Darlington gave it to the National Trust, but it had become dilapidated and was pulled down in 1960.

The best preserved and tallest surviving tower, although on the Stourhead National Trust estate in Wiltshire, is in Somerset – by just a few feet! King Alfred's Tower was built by Henry Hoare II in 1772 to commemorate King Alfred's victory over the Danes at the battle of Edington (Ethandune) in AD 878. The three-sided tower is 160ft high, with round angle-towers on each corner, and reputedly contains 1 million bricks. The 222 steps lead to a viewing platform of Chilmark stone.

During the Second World War the tower had an encounter with a low-flying Mosquito aircraft; the repairs to the tower can be seen about two-thirds of the way up, as the new brickwork is a lighter colour. As Mosquitos had a wooden fuselage and wings, the tower would have had the better of the exchange!

When the Ammerdown Park Tower (*see* entry 54) was opened with great ceremony in 1854, John Turner, a local quarry owner, was not happy. He had just lost a lawsuit with Lord Hylton and was determined upon revenge. Apparently Lord Hylton was an extremely shy and private man, so Turner decided to build a tower on his land at Faulkland (ST 738543), tall enough to overlook Ammerdown House and gardens and so annoy Lord Hylton by seeing all his comings and goings. Although only 20ft square, it soared 120ft to the first viewing platform; then to 138 and 150ft where there were a further two platforms, each partly cantilevered out, then finally to a 'crow's-nest' at 160ft surmounted by a flagstaff, flying Turner's colours at 175ft. To cover the cost of this monstrosity, Turner had a tearoom and dance hall built next to it, hoping to attract the local miners, but this failed. Turner's Tower, in about 1885, could have had no architect for it seems to have been structurally impossible, and not surprisingly it soon became unsafe and had to be partly demolished. After Turner's death in 1894, Lord Hylton's descendant bought the remains and converted the stump and the dance hall and tearoom into cottages, thus redeeming the family pride.

James Thomson certainly knew what he was writing about in 'The Seasons':

> . . . till by degrees the finished fabric rose,
> and bade him to be lord of all below.

Above: Alfred's Tower. *(Mike Jones)*

Below: Turner's Tower, *c.* 1886. *(Mike Jones)*

SOUTH PETHERTON

Petherton Bridge

It is difficult to imagine now that there is a bridge here with the traffic roaring past on the dual carriageway of the A303, but underneath flows the River Parrett. There was probably a Roman bridge here, for it is on the line of the Fosse Way (*see* entry 60) and there have been many bridges since.

The grieving or the benefactors?

Built into the north side of the western concrete abutment of the bridge is a relic of a previous bridge, showing two much-worn carved male and female figures, which were once on the end of a parapet of the former bridge. There is no record of their true origin or meaning: one story is that the figures once adorned an old chapel at Stoke sub Hamdon; another that they represent two children who were drowned by falling into the Parrett from an even older wooden bridge, replaced with a stone bridge by their grieving parents; yet another version is supported by Thomas Gerard who, writing in 1633, relates that it was 'a faire stone bridge, at the end of which I have seene graven on a stone the effigies of the founder and his wife, now much defaced by lewde people, and the memory of them for want of an inscription lost'. The truth is buried somewhere in these last two stories.

Also preserved beside this stone is another, formerly at the other end of the parapet, an early signpost inscribed thus:

THE RIG

HT HAND

ROADE

LEADDE

TO YEO

Either 'VIL' was never inscribed at the end or has been defaced, but the stonemason evidently could not adjust the size of his lettering to the width of the stone!

SPAXTON

The Abode of Love

During the early part of the nineteenth century 'Abodes of Love', or 'Agapemonies', had been established in France, Germany and the United States, but it was in Victorian England, of all places, where they had their strongest hold, flourishing in a remote part of Somerset for over a hundred years.

The Revd James Henry Prince (1811–99), a doctor of medicine and a clergyman of the Church of England, took up their ideas of 'spiritual wifehood' with himself as a 'heavenly bridegroom'; but for this he needed money. He married the very old but very wealthy Martha Freeman and then, when she died, the well-off Julia Starky, sister of one of his disciples, the Revd Mr Starky. (Many of the 600 Agapemonists* in this country were clergymen). Prince was staying in Taunton with three of his disciples, the Revd Lewis Price, the Revd George Thomas and Brother William Crabbe, when he met the five Nottridge sisters, each of whom had been left £6,000 by their

The Abode,
c. 1920.
(Mike Jones)

* The Agapemonists took their name from an old Roman pagan festival of love – the 'agapae'.

father. Prince was charismatic and he persuaded Harriet to marry Price, Agnes to marry Thomas and Clara to marry Crabbe – all in a few days! The three girls brought in £18,000, for everyone who became an Agapemonist had to make over all their worldly goods to the community.

Prince bought a twenty-bedroom house at Spaxton and built the chapel which became the principle room 'for there was a large red sofa beside the fire, red Persian carpets on the floor and red velvet curtains to the stained-glass lancet windows'. There was a billiard table, where

The Abode today.

both 'brothers' and 'sisters' played, with the cue rack beside the church fittings, these decorated with the sacred lamb and dove. A successful farm was established, with stables for the coach horses and cottages in which the majority of the community lived, for in 1870 there were 120 residents, of whom only 20 were male. Once there it was difficult for an individual to leave, having made over all his or her money, and this was became even more problematic after Elizabeth, the fourth of the Nottridge sisters, was 'rescued' by relatives, for Prince had two bloodhounds patrolling the grounds at night. When Prince set up the Abode he announced that he was the new Messiah, but after a while, his ageing 'soul wives' no longer pleasing him, he took Zoe, the 16-year-old daughter of a 'sister' to be his new 'bride of the lamb'. The image of 'spiritual brides' was only slightly dented when Zoe produced three children, and although Mr Starky and his wife left, the Abode survived and even grew in strength, bolstered by younger women – and their money – joining the community.

For some years before he died in 1899 Prince became deranged by his excesses, but did arrange for a successor, the Revd John Hugh Smyth-Pigott, 'a captivating and irresistibly good-looking young curate'. He had married Catherine Reynolds and together they reorganised the Abode, bringing order, financial stability and the twentieth century to the community, with cars, the telephone and electric light. Smyth-Pigott was even more debauched than Prince and he organised the community into three classes: 'helpmates of God' who did all the menial work but who could be promoted to the second class who did no work and were waited upon. Then there was the highest class (about thirty of the youngest and best-looking women) deemed fit to be 'soul brides' or 'brides of the lamb' for the Messiah and his disciples.

By this time, however, there was disquiet, not only in the village but throughout the country, about the conduct within this closed community. In 1906 the Bishop of Bath and Wells summoned Smyth-Pigott to appear before a Consistory Court to explain his conduct; he declined to attend, saying that he was the Messiah, and in 1909 he was defrocked. He took several 'brides', his wife, Catherine, seemingly compliant. The last was Ruth who bore him two sons, Power and Glory, and a daughter, Light. It is said that he had almost hypnotic charm and held complete sway over his flock. The goings-on, however, started to incense the local population, demonstrations were held outside the gates, and on several occasions the police had to be called in to keep order. Especially when Charles Read, a long-standing member of the Abode, was mistaken in the dark for Smyth-Pigott and was stripped, tarred and feathered by a gang of youths from Bridgwater.

The chapel today.

When Smyth-Pigott died in 1929 the Abode was in decline, although it was kept going by Ruth, but by the 1930s it had become a dreary home for disillusioned old women and a few disappointed girls; it closed in 1957 with only fifteen of the elderly remaining.

The house is still there, although much altered and the high surrounding walls have come down; the chapel became a workshop but today its lancet windows are boarded up. The children of the 'brides' are still remembered but perhaps the 'Abode of Love' itself will be recalled through the name of the local public house. This was formerly two cottages next to the Abode and someone had the wit, with tongue firmly in cheek, to name it the Lamb Inn!

STANDERWICK

Alfred's Stone

85
Map Ref
ST 828506

Did Alfred's Stone, or the Red Stone as it is sometimes called, mark the site of a 'Witenagemit' (Anglo-Saxon council or parliament) or, as oral tradition has it, was it where King Alfred met his council to plan the defeat of the Danes?

All that can now be seen poking up through the rough grass near Standerwick is quite small, for the reddish-coloured stone is only about 2ft wide and about the same to its curved top. It lies beside a track leading to a farm and the site does not appear to have any

Alfred's stone.

significance, such as at Cock Crowing Stone (*see* entry 96), for it is not near any crossroads and is certainly not on an eminence.

Perhaps the name Standerwick gives a clue to its origin, for 'wick' means a farmstead and 'stander', stoney or stones. Of course that could just imply that the farm had stoney ground but the countryside does not show this.

86
Map Ref
ST 600633

STANTON DREW

Stone Circles

The fifteenth-century stone bridge over the River Chew, with its two ribbed arches, makes a delightful entrance to the picturesque village of Stanton Drew, complete with old cottages and the handsome court of 1753. And, of course, there are the stone circles.

What is so curious about Stanton Drew is that so little is made of the stone circles, the stone rows and other nearby stones. Although under the guardianship of English Heritage and accessible to the public, perhaps it is because they are on private farmland. The approach to the stones, although signposted, is not easy and car parking is restricted; there are also no facilities and although explanatory leaflets are available there is an entry charge – £1 in the honesty box!

Although many of the stones forming the main circle, one of the largest in the country, have fallen, the size is awesome, and taken with

the two smaller circles, one of which almost touches the great circle, can compare with the sites on Salisbury Plain. True, their setting is not so grand or as well-researched as others, but recently a geophysical survey of the main circle was undertaken. A magnetometer survey revealed that the megalithic remains are only a ruin of what was once a site of far greater importance. Inside the main circle are nine concentric circles of highly elaborate pits and the stone circle itself is contained within an enclosure ditch; all are hidden under the pasture of the field. Such a site has a similarity with Woodhenge and the Sanctuary, near Avebury. Some of the visible stones are of dolomitic conglomerate, some are sandstone and others Jurassic limestone. The great circle is 120yds across and consists of twenty-four standing stones with an average height of 6ft; the smaller circle next to it has eight stones and is 30yds across while, in the adjoining field, the circle is 45yds across with twelve of its stones upright.

There are other stones in the vicinity and undoubtedly connected to the main site; the Cove with three stones, possibly a chambered tomb; two in a field called Middle Ham and Hauteville Quoit on the other side of the river, now prostrate and much depleted by being chipped away for road stone in the past.

Like so many other stone circles, the legend of merrymakers – a wedding party in this case, dancing on a Sunday and being turned to stone for their wickedness – surrounds these circles. However, the Hauteville Quoit (ST 601638) has a stranger tale. Sir John de Hauteville, a thirteenth-century knight who lived during the reign of King Henry III (1207–72), lies in effigy in St Andrew's Church in Chew Magna. According to Pevsner Sir John is 'a mysterious effigy' because of the way he is depicted. 'A giant of a man' was how he was described and he must have been to have thrown the Quoit (weighing many tons) from the top of Maes Knoll, about 2 miles away from where it lies today. A great story but how ever did it originate?

87
Map Ref
ST 204428

STOGURSEY

St Andrew's Church

The priory church of St Andrew at Stoke Courcey is so exceptional that one aspect of its fabric deserves a special mention. During restorations in the 1940s, the sloping floor of the crossing and of the chancel were exposed, so giving a superb prospect when looking from the nave to the Sanctuary. From the crossing the floor rises slightly up to the chancel, which slopes upward to five steps, then inclines to a further three steps, then yet again to the Sanctuary steps. This makes the floor of the Sanctuary some 10ft above that in the nave. Here the congregation has to look, almost neck-achingly, up to the Sanctuary, with the priest, of course, being able to look down on the length of the church. Few churches can match the awe-inspiring feeling of this vista.

And few churches retain a Sanctuary Ring. Here the old iron ring, about 6in in diameter, is secured to the south-eastern pillar of the crossing, and here in the Middle Ages a criminal could take sanctuary in the church after touching the ring – but he had to leave England within forty days. In extreme cases, provided they held on to the ring, they would be safe from their pursuers until a proper officer arrived to take them into custody. There were severe penalties for anyone on either side breaking these rules.

There is also a splendid brass chandelier in the church, made by John Bayley of Bridgwater in 1732. Many of the lovely chandeliers seen in West Country churches were made either in Bristol or Bridgwater.

Below, left: The view down from the Sanctuary.

Below, right: The Sanctuary Ring.

STOGURSEY

St Andrew's Well

At the end of Old Cross Street in Stogursey a cobbled alley leads down to a handsome stone archway, beyond which is a small court-yard where, on either side of the arch, are two covered cisterns, each enclosing a spring, the water issuing through three spouts into two troughs. Bearing the same name as the church, St Andrew's Well was regarded for many years as a holy well, probably because of the purity of the water (many village wells, espccially draw wells, were highly polluted by middens or privies). It was considered that the left-hand spring was best for drinking while the right-hand spring, because it was softer, was more suitable for washing.

In 1757 the Earl of Egremont had the springs enclosed as they are today, and an entrance arch erected with his coat of arms on its inner face. In 1847 the springs were described as providing the only good public drinking water in the village and had never been known to run dry. In 1870 the well was restored by Sir Peregrine Ackland, of Fairfield, whose coat of arms can be seen over the entrance arch.

St Andrew's Well.

STOLFORD

Mud Horses

Only two fishermen, Brendon and Adrian Sellick, now continue a centuries-old method of fishing, once common all along the north Somerset coast. At Stolford, the tide goes out nearly a mile and, within the tide lines, nets are strung out between fixed poles set upright on the shore, to catch the fish brought in by the high tide and strong tidal currents of the Bristol Channel. Flat fish, prawns and shrimps are caught and the nets have to be attended to on every suitable low tide.

However, on this stretch of coast, the foreshore does not just consist of rocks, but vast areas of deep clinging mud, almost impossible to walk over. So, long ago, 'mud horses' were devised: flat wooden sleds with upturned prows, and an open wooden super-structure which carried the nets and catch, and on which the fishermen could lean, both to support themselves on the mud and to push the sled forward. It is hard and dirty work and one wonders how much longer the custom will survive.

The prawns and shrimps are boiled in a copper and then drained in shallow, round baskets, each having a raised conical centre so that the cooked shellfish can cool and drain. These are made especially for this purpose by a Sedgemoor basket-maker.

Brendon Sellick demonstrating a mud horse – on dry land.

STREET

The Eureka

One of the most curious and intriguing inventions ever (and probably one of the most useless!) was the Latin verse machine of John Clark.

Born at Greinton, John Clark (1785–1852) lived with an uncle at Glastonbury before moving to Bridgwater in 1815, where he became a self-employed printer. It was not until 1830 that he conceived the idea for 'The Eureka' as he called the machine: an automatic, mechanical means of composing Latin hexameters (lines of verse consisting of six metrical feet). It was not completed until 1845, when Clark put it on display at the Egyptian Hall in London and a handbill circulated details of 'THE EUREKA, A MACHINE FOR MAKING LATIN VERSES EXHIBITED DAILY. From 12 to 5 and from 7 to 9 oClock, WITH ILLUSTRATIVE LECTURES. ADMITTANCE ONE SHILLING'. Clark made 'a handsome sum of money' from the exhibition and the resulting national interest, including an article in the *London Illustrated News*. He retired and wrote the definitive work on the machine: *General History and Description of a Machine for Composing Latin Hexameter Verses*.

Its working can be summarised best in the words of D.W. Blandford, writing in *Greece and Rome* in 1963:

The Eureka.
(Richard Clark)

> Externally the machine resembles an old-fashioned vending machine, with a word appearing in each of six slots. The mechanism works like a grandfather clock, by weights, pulleys and gearing, wound up with a clock key. Words are formed by a series of lettered staves which rest on stop wires projecting from revolving drums. The staves are vertical rods about 24 inches long, of which roughly the middle third is marked from bottom to top with twenty-seven letters or diphthongs – omitting W, and added AE and OE. In all there are forty-seven staves grouped behind the six slots as follows:
>
> No. of slot . . . 1 2 3 4 5 6
> No. of staves . . . 8 6 7 12 —

Thus in slot 1 it is possible to have a word of up to eight letters, in slot 2 a word of up to six letters, and so on. The staves are raised and lowered behind the slots, and their resting positions determine the letters which appear. The different resting positions are determined by stop wires on drums beneath. There are six drums in all – one for each slot – resembling so many mechanical hedgehogs. Each revolves on a horizontal axis, and running lengthways along each are numerous stop wires of different but carefully planned lengths, varying from 9 inches to less than half an inch. As the staves come to rest on these stop wires, the letters arranged by the inventor appear in the slot above. The shorter the wire, the farther the stave will drop, and the letter appearing in the slot will be that much later in the alphabet. The number of wires in a row varies according to the number of letters in the required word, each wire corresponding to one letter and the absence of a wire producing a blank. Each row of wires produces one word. The number of rows on each drum represents the number of possible words, viz:

No. of drum . . . 1 2 3 4 5 6
No. of rows . . . 13 16 17 18 19 20

Therefore in slot 1 it is possible to have fifteen different words, in slot 2 sixteen, and so on – making a total of 105. Each line producing a permutation of six of these words. The number of possible lines is, therefore, taking into account the repetition of one word on drum 3 – 26,265,600 words!

To ensure that each line is grammatically correct, all the words on any particular drum must be of the same part of speech, thus the word order being always the same, viz:

No. of drum . . .   1 2 3 4 5 6
Part of speech . . . Adjective Noun Adverb Verb Verb Adjective

Likewise, to ensure each line will scan, all the words on any particular drum must have the same metrical form.

The machine also had a musical box which played the National Anthem while the hexameter was being put together and when the line was to be broken up, 'Fly not Yet'!

It was eventually put on permanent display at the Crispen Hall Museum in Street, but when that closed it was put into the archive of Clark's Boot and Shoe Museum. It is hoped that it will be restored and again shown to the public.

Perhaps John Clark should best be remembered for another invention he patented – a method of impregnating cloth with rubber to make it waterproof – but he sold the rights of this to a certain Mr Mackintosh!

TATWORTH

Candle Auction

Candle auctions, where a short piece of candle is lit and the last bid before it goes out is accepted, were once fairly common throughout the country, but are now rare. Two are still carried on in Somerset, at the villages of Tatworth and Chedzoy.

When the common land at Tatworth was enclosed in 1819, one area, Stowell Mead, was excluded, with certain farmers within the parish having rights of grazing and rights to the watercress, which grew there in profusion. Because of administrative difficulties, it was agreed to let the meadow, on a yearly basis, to one farmer and the rent paid by him to be distributed equally to all those having rights.

The auction at Tatworth takes place on the first Tuesday after 6 April (conforming to the pre-Gregorian Calendar of 1752) and is now held at 7 p.m. in an upstairs room at Ye Olde Poppe Inn. One inch of tallow candle (wax is not allowed) is lit and after the door is locked the bidding commences; the last bid before the candle expires is successful. A fine is imposed on anyone arriving late or on anyone leaving their seat after the door is locked; besides those having rights, new members (cadets) can attend as well as the landlord who also has the right. The candle burns for anything between eight and seventy minutes and no one can leave the room for any reason while the candle is burning.

The auction at Chedzoy (ST 339374) is older, dating from the fifteenth century, and is held every twenty-one years (the next is in 2019) for a piece of land known as Church Acre. Only half an inch of tallow candle is used and the procedure is much the same as at Tatworth but with one great difference – it is not held in private. The use of the land is also different for here the field can be put to any agricultural use, including ploughing for arable purposes, but no permanent building can be erected. The auction used to take place at the manor house but is now held at the Manor House Inn, with the one held in 1967 being attended by over 300 people.

TAUNTON

Electricity Substations

In the 1920s Taunton's electricity supply had used a single-phase three-wire system, but in the early 1930s this was replaced by the more efficient three-phase system, which meant the digging up of Taunton's streets to lay the three-phase cables, and the replacement of all the electricity substations.

The new substations were 'tastefully' built of brick, with clay-tiled roofs, diamond-paned, leaded windows and fake exterior timbering, and looked for all the world like small detached garages for the mock-Tudor houses then being erected in the more affluent suburbs.

Dotted around the then out-skirts of the town, three of these sixty-year-old substations are still in use, reminding us that even in those far-off days public utilities liked to move with the times and build in a modern style.

The substation in East Reach.

93
Map Ref
ST 2224

TAUNTON

A Town sent to Coventry

When the Duke of Monmouth – the illegitimate son of Charles II by his mistress, Lucy Waters – landed at Lyme Regis on 11 June 1685, it was to claim the throne of England from his uncle, King James II. He proceeded to Taunton where he was welcomed with rejoicing by the populace, and was presented with a sword, a Bible and twenty-seven colours for his troops, sewn and given to him by twenty-seven young maidens dressed in white. Then, amid much jubilation, he proclaimed himself King.

Unfortunately, the support, both with men and money, was not forthcoming from the nobility or the local gentry, and when he met the Royalist forces at Westonzoyland (see entry 102) on 6 July, his mainly untrained and poorly armed troops were soundly beaten; the Duke fled, to be later captured and executed.

Retribution by summary hanging was quickly carried out on many of his followers, and when the harsh Judge Jeffreys came down from London, the more wealthy supporters were either heavily fined or had their property sequestrated, while many of the more humble soldiery were hanged or transported to the colonies.

For the support they had given the Duke, the people of Taunton were made to suffer badly and their disloyalty to the Crown was neither quickly forgiven nor forgotten. In fact, the town was ostracised and no subsequent king or queen visited Taunton for over 300 years. It is even said that when Queen Victoria passed through Taunton by train on her way west, she had all the blinds lowered as a sign of disapproval! Taunton only came out of the shadows in 1987, when an official visit was paid by Queen Elizabeth II.

Of course, Taunton had 'blotted its copybook' before – in 1497 it was here that Perkin Warbeck was proclaimed King!

TAUNTON

Ostler's Bell

On the wall by the side entrance to the Winchester Arms Hotel is a smooth stone with 'The Ostler's Bell' painted neatly on it. The bell pull has gone, but it is a delightful reminder of a more leisurely bygone age. A similar, very faded and almost illegible inscription can be seen beside the main entrance to the White Hart Hotel in Martock, although this does retain its highly polished bell pull.

94
Map Ref
ST 224245

The ostler's bell on the White Hart Hotel, Martock.

TAUNTON

Ramshorn Bridge

95
Map Ref
ST 216238

Now completely surrounded by suburbia, it is surprising that this little packhorse bridge has survived at all. Galmington stream has been diverted so it is a bridge over nothing which is surrounded by iron railings to prevent anyone crossing over it. The fact that it has no side walls does not necessarily mean that they have been demolished, for many packhorse bridges either had very low walls or no walls at all so as not to impede the ponies with their huge packs of wool slung on either side. But at least Ramshorn Bridge is still there, even if it cannot compare with the other more picturesque little packhorse

Above: Bench end at North Cadbury showing a packhorse crossing a bridge.

Right: Ramshorn Bridge.

bridges which survive throughout the county – at Allerford, Bruton, Bury, Dunster, Horner, Pensford, Queen Camel, Winsford and others. All are worth finding and walking across.

WAMBROOK

96

Map Ref
ST 302091

Cock Crowing Stone

Now almost completely buried beneath many years of ditch cleaning and road surfacing, is a large natural boulder which has always been known as Cock Crowing Stone. It is set in the verge of a minor road from Chard to Bewley Down where it is crossed by a narrow lane from Cotley to Wadeford.

On the north-east facing escarpment of the Blackdown Hills there were many such natural boulders, known as sarsens or silcretes, scattered on the surface where they were deposited during the thaw after the Ice Age. They were cleared from arable land and many were used to make hedges, while a few were put to use to mark boundaries or road junctions, such as those at Staple Fitzpaine (ST 264183) and Broadway (ST 320154). None, though, are recorded on the top of the Blackdown Hills, so it is almost certain that Cock Crowing Stone was brought here from some way away and placed here for a purpose. Was it the Romans, for an old name for this crossroads is 'Maximus Cross', or was it a boundary mark on the former boundary between Somerset and Devon? However, it is quite possible that, like a similar stone at Looe in Cornwall, the origin of the name has something to do with Christ's words at the Last Supper. The stone at Looe is said to turn three times on hearing a cock crow – hence its name 'Cock Crow Stone'.

One of four silcretes by the crossroads at Staple Fitzpaine.

WAMBROOK

Red Post

97

Map Ref
ST 305082

Red Post.

During the eighteenth and early nineteenth centuries, convicted felons had to walk from the court to their place of imprisonment or, if sentenced to transportation, to the nearest port. Eighteen miles was the regulation distance to be walked each day, the authorities making arrangements with farmers and landowners for a barn to be made available thereabouts as a shelter for the night. The guards accompanying the prisoners were often illiterate and unable to read the names on the finger posts, so when they had to turn off the road to find such barns, the post was painted red.

On the road from Chard to Wambrook (a main route to Exeter before the era of the turnpike roads) there was such a post where the lane from Cotley crossed to Palfrey's Lane. About a mile down this lane was a barn, also colour-washed red (ST 308093). Even after the barn was converted into a small cottage it was still painted red and known as 'Red Barn'; it was demolished in 1940 after being empty for many years. The signpost continues to be painted red by the local authority and the crossroads has become known as Red Post.

On the road from Langport to Sherborne there was another red post which directed the warders guarding the convicts down the road to Yeovil and the County Gaol at Ilchester, about 1½ miles away (the gaol is now demolished). The finger post has been superseded by modern road signs but the crossroads is known as Red Post Cross (ST 517253).

Two Red Posts survive in Dorset – one on a main road.

98
Map Ref
ST 550453

WELLS

A Long Jump

At the Rome Olympics in 1960, Wells's Mary Rand, then Mary Bignal, was expected to win the Ladies' Long Jump, but was only ninth. However, four years later in Tokyo, she made her four best jumps ever to take the Gold, the first British woman to have won a track or field event. She later married again, to the American decathlete Bill Toomey.

A long jump.

Set into the pavement on the north side of the Market Square at Wells is the Olympic symbol of five linked rings, a measured distance and a plaque, all of brass set into granite. The plaque records the prowess of one of Wells' most distinguished daughters and is a lasting tribute to her achievement:

This represents the world record Ladies' Long Jump, made by Mary Bignal Rand of this city, to win the Gold Medal at the Olympic Games in Tokyo in 1964. It is 22 feet 2¼ inches long and is placed here in admiration of her achievement. Presented by T.W.W.

WELLS

The Cathedral's Astronomical Clock

99
Map Ref
ST 551458

In the north transept of the Cathedral Church of St Andrew can be seen what is probably the second oldest clock in the world, with the automata above it and, to one side, a 'Jack' who strikes the hours and quarters. These, and the clock on the outside of the north transept together with its two Jacks, are all worked, via a system of rods, wires, pulleys and levers, from the clock mechanism high up in what is now the verger's office. All date from between 1344 and 1392, although the clock mechanism was replaced in 1880, with the original being restored and now in the Science Museum in London.

Below, left: The clock face, c. 1910.

Below, right: Jack Blandifer, c. 1924.

Before Copernicus (1473–1553) discovered that the earth circled the sun, it was believed that the earth was the centre of the universe and that the sun went round the earth. The 'astronomical' clock reflects this Ptolemic theory, so besides showing the time it also gives a lesson in this belief. In Roman numerals the outer circle shows the day as two twelve-hour cycles from noon to midnight on the right and from midnight to noon on the left, with noon and midnight shown as a cross. A golden sun traverses this circle giving the time in hours. A second circle is divided by Arabic numerals into sixty minutes with a small golden sun giving the minute of the hour. The innermost circle shows, in an anticlockwise direction, the thirty days of a lunar month, with a pointer set in a crescent moon, moving clockwise to indicate the day of the month after the new moon. As the moon plate, with the pointer, revolves, so a hole cut in the plate shows a golden moon waxing and waning, as well as its position in the heavens. In the very centre of the clock is a small ball, representing the earth as the centre of the universe.

The automaton above the clock face is a delightful piece of medieval fun, and has two knights on horseback charging out from one side of a castellated castle and another two charging out from the other, one of which is knocked back off his horse at every circuit. This spectacle used only to be seen on the hour, but in 1968, aided by an electric motor (the only modern addition to the complete mechanism), it was made to appear on every quarter, although for fewer circuits.

The Jack sitting in his sentry box, strikes the quarters on two bells with the heels of his shoes and the hours on a bell hanging in front of him with a hammer held in his right hand; with each strike of the hour bell his head moves slightly from side to side. Why this Jack should be called Jack Blandifer is not recorded, only that the wooden figure is contemporary with the clock, although he was repainted in the seventeenth century with a beard and moustache of that period.

The clock outside the north transept also once showed a 24-hour face with two twelve-hour cycles and just one hour hand. However, in about 1830 this face was replaced with a twelve-hour dial and an hour and minute hand. The two Jacks above it, two knights in probably fifteenth-century armour, strike the quarters with their halberds (a combined spear and battle-axe).

There is no firm evidence to show who actually made this magnificent piece of medieval craftsmanship. The oldest clock mechanism is at Salisbury Cathedral, although no clock face has survived. In the West Country there are also astronomical clocks at Exeter Cathedral, Sherborne Abbey, Wimborne Minster and Ottery St Mary, this last having the oldest mechanism still working the clock face.

WELLS

The Chapter House Steps

100
Map Ref
ST 551458

Wells Cathedral is probably the most beautiful of all English cathedrals with its impressive West Front and the awe-inspiring, intersecting ogee curves of the crossing tower. The Chapter House, however, is breathtaking in its glory, with the central pier expanding, fountainlike, into thirty-six ribs and with five shafts supporting the vaulting from the corners. No description can possibly do justice to its beauty and grandeur but the steps up to it from the Lady Chapel, then on up to the Chain Bridge, deserve more than a mere mention.

It is not just that this flight of stone stairs has been worn hollow by countless feet over the past 600 years, it is the way they sweep down from the Chain Bridge and these being then joined by the steps coming down from the Chapter House. Seen from the bottom they give the impression of two stone glaciers converging on one another, merging and then flowing on down as one. Simple stone steps but they add to the glory that is Wells.

The Chapter House steps from *Highways and Byways of Somerset.*

WELLS

St Andrew's Well

101
Map Ref
ST 552459

Just to the east of Wells Cathedral and within the gardens of the Bishop's Palace, is a lake (there is no other word for it) known as St Andrew's Well, taking its name from the Cathedral Church of St Andrew. This is really a 'collecting pond', constructed during the nineteenth century, gathering the water from five springs which erupt here and from which, of course, the city of Wells took its name. The amount of water surging up from the underlying rock is immense, approximately 1,152,000 gallons a day, spilling over an imposing waterfall into the moat surrounding the Bishop's Palace.

Wells Cathedral
reflected in the
still waters of
St Andrew's Well.

These springs once gave the town its supply of pure water, with some still flowing down the sides of the High Street. There was a little waterwheel and pump which supplied the palace, and although now in a dilapidated condition, it is, hopefully, soon to be restored. No photograph can do the well justice, but the palace grounds are occasionally opened to the public.

WESTONZOYLAND

A Young Heroine

102

Map Ref
ST 350348

After the battle of Sedgemoor on 6 July 1685 and Monmouth's defeat, capture and execution on 27 July, a terrible vengeance was exacted on the West Country and all of Monmouth's supporters – over 300 – were hanged, drawn and quartered, and 600 others transported for life.

Foremost in ruthlessness and cruelty, even surpassing that of Judge Jeffreys, was Colonel Percy Kirke and his 'Lambs', so called not as a sick joke, which it was, but because of his troop's insignia – the paschal lamb. They had previously served in Tangiers and brought back to England the brutish methods used to deal with their enemies;

for they never paid in full for any goods or services and, it was said, 'made an entire bawdy house of ye West of England, forcing and enticing the wives and daughters of such as were accounted nonconformist'.

Colonel Kirke led by example, for when he was in Crewkerne summarily executing rebels, 'an innkeeper's daughter fell down on her knees in floods of tears, begging he would be a means of saving her father's life. He promised, on condition that she would yield herself to him. She consented, hoping thus to save

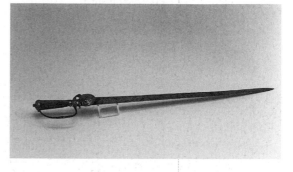

her father's life. On getting out of bed the next morning she saw her father hanging from the inn's sign post.' This example makes the case of Mary Bridges all that more remarkable.

Mary Bridge's sword. *(Somerset Museum Service)*

Mrs Bridges lived in a substantial house in Westonzoyland (now demolished and replaced by a red-brick house but retaining the original 1685 Hamstone door frames and lintel). It is not known if her husband had been a Monmouth supporter, but all the same, she was obliged to have several of Kirke's officers billeted in her home. One night one of these officers tried to rape Mrs Bridges; her 12-year-old daughter, Mary, coming upon the act and desperate to save her mother, drew the officer's sword – he being otherwise engaged – and ran him through. His fellow officers, outraged at this murder, dragged Mary for summary trial before Colonel Kirke. Surprisingly, he so admired Mary's spirit that he acquitted her of any crime and gave her the sword to pass down to her descendants as a memento of her courage.

In 1932 two of Mary's descendants, Mrs P.M. Wright and Miss Mary Bridges, gave the sword to Somerset, where it can be seen today in the County Museum at Taunton.

WINSFORD

Caratacus Stone

103
Map Ref
SS 890336

Why this stone from the Dark Ages (AD 450 to 650) should have been set up near the crossroads high on Winsford Hill is something that will never be known, any more than who exactly the stone commemorates. As the inscription cut into the stone is not complete it is uncertain whether it reads 'Carataci Nepus' or 'Caranaci Nepus' (kinsman of Caratacus or Caranacus).

Right: The Smithy Bridge, Winsford.

Below: The Caractacus Stone in its shelter.

When Cara(c)tacus – that doughty leader of the West Britons opposing the Romans – was eventually captured in AD 50 and taken to Rome, the Emperor Claudius was so impressed by his courage and bearing that he gave him his freedom. It would be good to think that if he came back to Britain it was to West Somerset where he brought his family to found a small dynasty here.

The stone is now protected by a 6ft-square, open-sided stone shelter which, although detracting from its remoteness and sense of history, does at least save it from the cattle and ponies otherwise using it as a rubbing post.

WINSHAM

104
Map Ref
ST 373065

For Automobilists

On 14 June 1904 a group of 'automobilists' met at Glastonbury to consider the formation of a motor club. Consequently the Somerset Automobile Club was set up and is still going strong one hundred years later.

In the beginning the club was instrumental in erecting, at their own expense, signs to warn the rare motorist of dangers on the road such as steep hills, blind corners and villages. Thirty-six of these signs were accepted by the County Council in 1907, which the club also had to erect, but on the insistence that the cost of any future signs would have to be met from the rates. Two were ordered by Chard Rural District Council in 1911 to be put up on the road from Chard to Beaminster where it went through Winsham and these are still in place, with their original 'Winsham Please Drive Slowly' beneath a triangle bearing the letters SAC. The 'Thank You' on the reverse is now painted out – cars are now going too fast for such niceties as that!

Please drive
slowly – in 1911.

105
Map Ref
ST 539480

WOOKEY

The Witch

On entering the second of the caves at Wookey Hole one is confronted by a strangely shaped stalagmite which, with a little imagination, could resemble a wizened face, with, close by, a much smaller stalagmite which could well be a little dog lying down. Legends, of course, have grown up around them: about a thousand years ago there lived in the cave a once-beautiful old woman who, because she lived alone (except for her dog) in a very unusual place, came to be thought of by the local villagers as a witch, with all the evils they suffered being attributed to her. When approached, the old woman would scuttle off down a dark passage, later known as Hell's Ladder, which the villagers were afraid to enter. At last they asked the Church for help and a monk, Father Bernard, was sent from Glastonbury to exorcise the evil. The woman fled, as usual, down

Wookey Hole Caves. *(Wookey Hole Caves Ltd)*

Hell's Ladder, but the monk, holding his crucifix high, followed her. He sprinkled her and her familiar (the dog) with holy water and they turned to stone. It is interesting that when the first archaeologist to really explore the caves, Herbert Balch, entered the third cave he found the bones of a woman, a dog, a sacrificial dagger and a round crystalline ball made smooth by much handling – the crystal ball of a magician!

There was also the story of King Arthur slaying the witch 'who lived in the cave at the Head of the Stream of Sorrow in the confines of Hell'. Wookey Hole certainly has a deep river flowing through the immense caverns it has carved for itself over countless millennia – sombre, almost dreadful, places where the thought of diving through those dark waters (as the cave explorers do) sends shivers down one's spine. Strangely, these caverns do not feel claustrophobic, although it is pleasant to come out into the light and see the River Axe emerging tranquilly from its underground womb. (This is just the place to encourage purple passages of prose!)

Outside there is an informative small museum explaining the caves' geology and prehistoric remains found in them; demon-strations of making paper by hand in the old way, and the recreation of bygone pierhead entertainments. Sadly, Titania's Palace, a doll's house built by a local craftsman in 1907 and given by Sir Neville Wilkman of Wookey to his 3-year-old daughter in 1923, can no longer be seen. Reputedly the world's largest and most important miniature house and contents, it was sold to a foreign collector some years ago.

The Witch of Wookey. *(Wookey Hole Caves Ltd)*

BIBLIOGRAPHY AND SOURCES

Books & Articles

(Unless otherwise stated place of publication is London.)

Atthill, R. (ed.), *Mendips. A New Study*, Newton Abbot, David & Charles, 1970

Blandford, D.W., *Greece and Rome Vol. x 1*, Oxford, Clarendon Press, 1963

Byford, E., *Somerset Curiosities*, Wimborne, Dovecote Press, 1989

Cameron, K., *English Place Names*, Methuen, 1961

Chard History Group, *The Roads, Canal and Railways of Chard*, 2001

Coleman-Cooke, P., *Exmoor National Park*, HMSO, 1970

Coysh, A.W., Mason, E.J. and Waite, V., *The Mendips*, Robert Hale, 1977

Cresswell, W.H.P., Revd, *Dunmonia and the Valley of the River Parrett*, Taunton, Wessex Press, 1922

Hadfield, J., *The Shell Guide to England*, Michael Joseph, 1970

Hamilton, R., *Now I Remember*, Pan, 1964

Hawkins, D., *Avalon and Sedgemoor*, Newton Abbot, David & Charles, 1976

Headley, G. and Meulenkemp, W., *Follies*, Jonathan Cape, 1989

Hoskins, L., *History of Tatworth and Forton*, Tatworth & Forton, 1975

Hutton, E., *Highways and Byways of Somerset*, Macmillan, 1912

Jelly, N., *St Patrick's Somerset Birthplace*, Cary Valley Historical Society, 1975

Jenkins, S., *England's Thousand Best Churches*, Penguin, 1999

Jervoise, E., *The Ancient Bridges of the South of England*, Architectural Press, 1930

Kille, H.J., *Hobby-Horses of the West Country*, Proceedings, Somerset Archaeological & Natural History Society, Vol. LXXVII, 1931

Knight, F.A., *Cambridge County Geographies, Somerset*, Cambridge, CUP, 1909

Legg, P., *So Merry Let Us Be*, Somerset County Council Library Service, 1986

Little, B., *Bath Portrait*, Bristol, Butleigh Press, 1972

Mabey, R., *Flora Britanica*, Sinclair-Stevenson, 1996

McCormick, D., *Temple of Love*, Jarrold, 1962

Mee, A., *Somerset*, Hodder & Stoughton, 1945

Miles, S., 'Oil at Kilve', in *Somerset Industrial Archaeological Society Bulletin*, 70, 1995

Murless, B.J., 'John Board. A Sedgemoor Man and Company', in *Somerset Industrial Archaeological Society Bulletin*, 65, 1994

Neale, F. and Lovell, A., *Wells Cathedral Clock*, Wells Cathedral Publications, 1998

Newman, P., *Bath*, Cambridge, Pevensey Press, 1978

Orwin, C.S. and Sellick, R.J., *The Reclamation of Exmoor Forest*, Newton Abbot, David & Charles, 1970

Palmer, K., *Somerset Folklore*, Batsford, 1976

Pevsner, N., *Buildings of England. North Somerset and Bristol*, Penguin, 1958

Pevsner, N., *Buildings of England. South and West Somerset*, Penguin, 1958

Prudden, H., *Geology and Landscape of Taunton Deane*, Taunton Deane Borough Council, 2001

Sitwell, E., *Bath*, Faber & Faber, 1932 (Redcliffe Press, Bristol, 1983)

Sykes, H., *Celtic Britain*, Cassell, 2001

Thomas, B., 'The Forgotten Spa', in *Somerset Magazine*, May 1995

Tongue, R.L., *Somerset Folklore*, The Folklore Society, 1968

Waite, V., *Portrait of the Quantocks*, Robert Hale, 1972

Walker, M., *Old Somerset Customs*, Bristol, Redcliffe Press, 1984

Warren, D., 'Lilstock Harbour', in *Somerset Industrial Archaeological Society Bulletin*, 52, 1989

Watts, M., *Somerset Windmills*, Keynsham, Agrephicus Press, 1975

Church Leaflets

St Mary Magdalen, Chewton Mendip
St Bartholomew, Crewkerne
St Mary, Croscombe
St Culbone, Culbone
St Martin of Tours, Fiddington
Friends Meeting House, Long Sutton
St Andrew, Mells
St Peter and St Paul, Muchelney
St Michael, North Cadbury
St Peter and St Paul, North Curry
All Saints, Nynehead
St Dubricus, Porlock
St Andrew, Stogursey

ACKNOWLEDGEMENTS

Ishould like to thank sincerely all those who allowed me to use their research, gave me information or permitted me to visit their properties, where I was invariably made welcome. I must also thank those who nudged my memory or pointed me in the right direction – if I have overlooked anyone it is because my memory needs further nudging!

Judith Bell, Administrator, Bath Preservation Trust; Hilary Binding, Carhampton; Mr M. and Mrs Isabel Briggs, Midford Archaeological and Natural History Society; Sandy Buchanan, Ashcott; Roger Carter, Curator, D. Cavender, Dowlish Wake; Chard Museum; Sally Chadwick, Doddington; Richard Clark, Street; Ian Clarke, Nether Stowey; Don Coombes, Pawlett; Hilary Cumming, Whitestaunton; Sue Eckersley, Wellington; Tom Flook, Pawlett; R.N. Green, Curry Rivel; David Greenfield, Taunton; Colonel David Hunt, Wokingham; Mike Jones, Taunton; Peter Legg, Harbourmaster, Burnham-on-Sea; Fred Look, Meare; Daniel Medley, Marketing, Wookey Hole Caves; Peter Milton, Orchardleigh; Brian Murless, Archivist, Somerset Industrial Archaeological Society; Angela Naunton Davies, Lopen; Catherine Oakes, Landmark Trust; John Overton, Bath; Parochial Church Council, Fiddington; Mrs B.M. Pon, Chaffcombe; Lorna Prudden, Montacute; Richard Read, Manager, NatWest Bank, Chard; Roy Rice, Banwell; R.J. Rogers, Administrator, Wells Cathedral; Marion Shaw, Warden, Bishop's Palace, Wells; Valerie Sherwin, Moorland Mousie Trust; Betty Sparkes, Nynehead; W.P.H. Speke, Rowlands, Ilton; W.A.C. Theed, Combe Sydenham, Monksilver; Richard Willey, Taunton.